RESERVOIR DOGS
and
TRUE ROMANCE

by the same author

PULP FICTION

RESERVOIR DOGS

and

TRUE ROMANCE

Screenplays by

Quentin Tarantino

GROVE PRESS
New York

Reservoir Dogs first published in Great Britain in 1994 by Faber and Faber Limited; *True Romance* first published in Great Britain in 1994 by Faber and Faber Limited.

First Grove Press edition published in 1995.

Printed in the United States of America

FIRST EDITION

Library of Congress Cataloging-in-Publication Data
[Reservoir dogs]
Reservoir dogs; and, True romance: screenplays / Quentin Tarantino. —1st ed.
ISBN 0-8021-3355-X
1. Motion picture plays. I. Tarantino, Quentin. True romance. II. Title. III. Title:
True romance.
PN1997.A1T287   1995   791.43'75—dc20   95-19619

Grove Press
841 Broadway
New York, NY 10003

10 9 8 7 6 5 4 3 2 1

Contents

Quentin Tarantino (photo by Paul Joyce)

Quentin Tarantino: Answers First, Questions Later

Quentin Tarantino was born in Knoxville, Tennessee, in 1963, the year when Monte Hellman's *Back Door to Hell* and *Flight to Fury*, Don Siegel's *The Killers*, and Sergio Leone's *A Fistful of Dollars* were also in gestation – as Tarantino himself could probably tell you. The writer/director of *Reservoir Dogs* (1992) and *Pulp Fiction* (1990), as well as the writer of *True Romance* (1993) and *Natural Born Killers* (1994), Tarantino is the most extreme instance of a movie-struck kid who has parlayed his obsession with cheap thrillers and Westerns into a career at a time when both forms are being reinvented and revitalized by Hollywood.

Tarantino was raised by his mother in Southern California and received his movie education at the Carson Twin Cinema, Scottsdale, and later as an employee of Video Archives, Manhattan Beach, where he worked while training as an actor. His scripts pullulate with references to his movie diet during those days. The story of two kids, Clarence (Christian Slater) and Alabama (Patricia Arquette), on the run with a cache of cocaine they've offloaded from the Mob, *True Romance*, directed by Tony Scott, is set up by Tarantino as a self-conscious analogue to Terrence Malick's *Badlands*, replete with the same Erik Satie theme and a gauche voice-over by the female lead.

The point is that Tarantino is not so much a post-modern *auteur* as a *post*-post-modern one, for he is feverishly interested in pop-cultural artefacts and ideas (television, rock music, comics, and junk food, as well as movies) that themselves spring from earlier incarnations or have already been mediated or predigested. Because *Badlands* was made with *They Drive By Night*, *You Only Live Once*, *Gun Crazy*, and James Dean in mind, *True Romance* has a double frame of reference. In *Reservoir Dogs* – Tarantino's update on Stanley Kubrick's *The Killing* and/or Larry Cohen's *Q* – the pre-heist debate about the possible meanings of Madonna's 'Like a Virgin', as implausible as it is funny, is an anti-intellectual demystification of Madonna's much chewed-over status as a post-feminist icon in books like *Madonnarama: Essays on Sex and Popular Culture*. It's not Madonna that concerns Tarantino in this scene – but what Madona has come to represent.

All of which might seem like mere dressage for Tarantino's tough, cynical, and exuberantly amoral genre-bending scripts. Except that his appreciation of pop ephemera is as central to his movies – you could say it is the world they move in – as their rabidly talky flow, their intricately structured plots, their casual explosions of violence, and their reverse psychology. (Brought together in anonymity, for example, *Reservoir Dogs'* hoods form immediate allegiances, while the coolest among them turns out to be a psychopathic killer and the angriest the most professional.) That delight in contradiction is really Tarantino's calling card, for he writes pulp movies for audiences who want more than mere visceral thrills, who may not have read much Tolstoy, and even less Michael Crichton or John Grisham, but who might figure out how bloody a 'Douglas Sirk steak' can be, or the qualitative difference between *Bewitched* and *I Dream of Jeannie* – to cite Tarantino's *Pulp Fiction*. This was the script he had just finished writing, for himself to direct, when we talked, in May 1993.

GRAHAM FULLER: *When you started writing scripts, was it as a means to becoming a director or because you had specific stories you wanted to tell as a screenwriter?*

QUENTIN TARANTINO: I've never considered myself a writer writing stuff to sell, but as a director who writes stuff for himself to direct. The first script I ever did was *True Romance*. I wrote it to do it the way the Coen Brothers did *Blood Simple*, and I almost directed it. Me and a friend, Roger Avary, were going to raise about $1.2 million, form a limited partnership and then go off and make the movie. We worked on it for three years, trying to get it off the ground like that, and it never worked. I then wrote *Natural Born Killers*, again hoping to direct it myself, this time for half-a-million dollars – I was shooting lower and lower. After a year and a half I was no further along than at the beginning. It was then out of frustration that I wrote *Reservoir Dogs*. I was going to go really guerrilla style with it, like the way Nick Gomez did *Laws of Gravity*. I'd lost faith in anyone giving me money – and then that's *when* I got the money.

GF: *What was your response to relinquishing* True Romance *and* Natural Born Killers *as scripts you would direct yourself?*

QT: After *Reservoir Dogs* I was offered both of them to direct. The producers who had *Natural Born Killers* – before Oliver Stone acquired it – tried like hell to talk me into directing it. Tony Scott and Bill Unger had *True Romance*. I had convinced Tony to direct it, but Bill was saying, 'Look, Quentin, would you be interested in doing this as a follow-up to *Reservoir Dogs?*' And my answer was no. I didn't want to do either one of them because they were both written to be my first film and by then I'd made my first film. I didn't want to go backwards and do old stuff. I think of them as like old girlfriends: I loved them but I didn't want to marry them any more. The thing that I am the happiest about is that the first film of mine produced was one that I directed.

GF: *How had you originally gone about positioning yourself in the industry?*

QT: During the time I wrote these things, I wasn't anywhere near the industry. Eventually, what got me inside was moving to Hollywood and making some friends who were film-makers. One of them was Scott Speigel, who had just written the Clint Eastwood movie, *The Rookie* [1990], and people were calling him to write things he didn't have time to do, so he would suggest me. The next thing I knew, I was sending out *True Romance* and *Natural Born Killers* as audition scripts and, little by little, I started doing a little rewrite at this company, doing a little dialogue polishing at that one.

GF: *You say you're not a writer, but the narratives of each of your scripts is very carefully crafted and rich in imagery. You establish your characters very fast.*

QT: I'm not trying to be falsely modest. I am a pretty good writer – but I always think of myself as a director.

GF: *In the* Natural Born Killers *script you wrote in a lot of the camera directions, so it was clearly a blueprint for a film you'd direct yourself. I remember Ken Russell saying he gets irritated when he sees scripts telling him where to put the camera.*

QT: Writing for somebody else and writing a movie for yourself to do are completely different. I'm not bagging on screenwriters, but if I was a full-on writer, I'd write novels.

GF: *You've talked about directors that have influenced you – including Samuel Fuller, Douglas Sirk, and Jean-Pierre Melville – but were you also influenced by specific screenwriters or novelists?*

QT: I think Robert Towne is one screenwriter who deserves every little bit of the reputation he has. I'm also a fan of Charles B. Griffith, who used to write for Roger Corman. But most of my writing heroes are novelists. When I wrote *True Romance*, I was really into Elmore Leonard. In fact, I was trying to write an Elmore Leonard novel as a movie, though I'm not saying it's as good.

GF: *What about earlier writers? Is your script for* Pulp Fiction *modelled on Cain, Chandler, and Hammett?*

QT: I don't know how much I am actually influenced by those guys, but I have read them all and I like them. The idea behind *Pulp Fiction* was to do a *Black Mask* movie – like that old detective story magazine. But I just finished the script and it's really not like that at all; it kind of went somewhere else. Two other writers I'm crazy about are Ben Hecht and Charles MacArthur, both as playwrights and as screenwriters. In fact, on the first page of *Pulp Fiction*, I describe two characters talking in 'rapid-fire motion, like in *His Girl Friday*'.

GF: *How do your screenplays evolve?*

QT: One of the main things I like to do with my scripts is monkey with structure a little bit. I always know the structure I am going to employ in advance, and all the whys and the wherefores of the story when I start writing, but there's always some unanswered questions, ideas I want to explore. I don't know how effective they're going to be, but I want to try them out. When I start writing I let the characters take over. If you read my scripts, you'll see that the dialogue scenes just go on and on and on. I never went to a screenwriting or creative writing class, but I did study acting for about six years and I actually approach writing the way an actor approaches acting.

GF: *Do you write in a linear way?*

QT: I have to write from beginning to end because the characters are kind of telling the story.

GF: True Romance's *narrative is linear, but with your script for* Natural Born Killers, *you wove in a lot of flashbacks and a long sequence involving a tabloid-TV-film-in-progress. Then you made another leap forward with* Reservoir Dogs, *which has a kind of dovetailed structure.*

QT: *True Romance* had a more complicated structure to start with, but when the producers bought the script they cut-and-pasted it into a linear form. The original structure was also an answers-first, questions-later structure, like *Reservoir Dogs*. Thinking back on it, that version probably wasn't the most effective script that I've done, but I still think it would have worked. Tony [Scott] actually started putting it together that way in the editing room, but he said it didn't work for him.

I guess what I'm always trying to do is use the structures that I see in novels and apply them to cinema. A novelist thinks nothing of starting in the middle of a story. I thought that if you could figure out a cinematic way to do that, it would be very exciting. Generally, when they translate novels to movies, that's the first stuff that goes out. I don't do this to be a wise guy or to show how clever I am. If a story would be more dramatically engaging if you told it from the beginning, or the end, then I'd tell it that way. But the *glory* is in pulling it off my way.

GF: *When you sat down to write* Reservoir Dogs, *did you have a structure or a stratagem in your head?*

QT: Definitely. I wanted the whole movie to be about an event we don't see, and I wanted it all to take place at the rendezvous at the warehouse – what would normally be given ten minutes in a heist film. I wanted the whole movie to be set there and to play with a real-time clock as opposed to a movie clock ticking. I also wanted to introduce these guys in a series of chapters. Like, when you're reading a book, you're reading about Moe, Larry and Curly doing something in chapters one, two, and three, and then chapter four is about Moe five years before. Then, when that chapter is over, you're back in the main thrust of the action again, but now you know a little bit more about this guy than you did before.

GF: *Did* Reservoir Dogs *go through rewrites?*

QT: Not really. I wrote it real quick, and six months after I wrote it, we were shooting it. After I did the first draft, the big change I made was to include the scene where Mr Orange is in the bathroom telling his story – that whole undercover-cop training sequence. I had written it earlier and then, when I was putting the script together, I thought, 'No one cares about this; they want to get back to the warehouse.' So I left it out and put it in my drawer. But when we were trying to get the movie made, I dug it out and read it and I went, 'Quentin, are you insane? This is really good. You've got to put this in.' That was the only major change to the second draft.

I also kept changing who said what in the opening scene. That was the thing that went through the most metamorphosis. At one time, Mr

Blonde made this speech, and another time Mr White said it, and so-and-so said this and so-and-so said that. I just kept switching speeches all the time. It's really funny, because when I look at it now, it doesn't look like it went through all that. But maybe it was good that it did – because all the right people ended up saying all the right things.

GF: *Did you have to fix things during shooting at all?*

QT: The only thing I did was a little polish after auditions, because auditioning shows you what lines don't work. So I got rid of them. Also, actors will come in and either improvise deliberately or they'll accidentally say something and it's funny.

GF: *I don't know if you've ever seen Michael Powell and Emeric Pressburger's* The Life and Death of Colonel Blimp . . .

QT: I never have – I've always wanted to.

GF: *The key event in the first half of the film is a duel between Roger Livesey and Anton Walbrook. There's a great deal of rigmarole leading up to it concerning the rules and codes of duelling. Then, just at the moment the duel is about to start, the camera cranes away from it and you never actually see it. It functions in the film in the same way the heist functions in* Reservoir Dogs. *My question is: do you consider omission part of the art of screenwriting? Is what you leave out as crucial as what you put in?*

QT: I completely think so. To me, it even applies to the way you frame a shot. What you don't see in the frame is as important as what you do see. Some people like to show everything. They don't want the audience to have a second guess about anything; it's *all* there. I'm not like that. I've seen so many movies that I like playing around with them. Pretty much nine out of ten movies you see let you know in the first ten minutes what kind of movie it's going to be, and I think the audience subconsciously reads this early ten-minute message and starts leaning to the left when the movie is getting ready to make a left turn; they're predicting what the movie is going to do. And what I like to do is use that information against them.

GF: *Do you feel that your screenplays provide a kind of legitimate forum for violence?*

QT: I don't quite look at it like that. I don't take the violence very seriously. I find violence very funny, and especially in the stories that I've been telling recently. Violence is part of this world and I am drawn to the outrageousness of real-life violence. It isn't about people lowering people from helicopters on to speeding trains, or about terrorists hijacking something or other. Real-life violence is, you're in a restaurant and a man and his wife are having an argument and all of a sudden the guy gets so mad at her, he picks up a fork and stabs her in the face. That's really crazy and comic-bookish – but it also *happens*; that's how real violence comes kicking and screaming into your perspective in real life. I am interested in the act, in the explosion, and in the entire aftermath of that. What do we do after this? Do we beat up the guy who stabbed the woman? Do we separate them? Do we call the cops? Do we ask for our money back because our meal has been ruined? I am interested in answering all those questions.

GF: *What about the visual aesthetics of violence, which seem to be writ large in your films? In John Woo's films, for instance, the violence is pleasurable to watch if you accept it as stylized comic-strip violence.*

QT: Well, like I say, I get a kick out of violence in movies. The worst thing about movies is, no matter how far you can go, when it comes to violence you are wearing a pair of handcuffs that novelists, say, don't wear. A writer like Carl Hiassen can do whatever he wants. The more outrageous, the better for his books. In movies, you don't really have that freedom.

GF: *When I asked you if your films provide a legitimate forum for violence, what I meant was that – within reason, obviously – it can be acceptable to see on screen that which is unpalatable in real life.*

QT: Oh, I completely agree with that. To me, violence is a totally aesthetic subject. Saying you don't like violence in movies is like saying you don't like dance sequences in movies. I do like dance sequences in movies, but if I didn't, it doesn't mean I should stop dance sequences from being made. When you're doing violence in movies, there's going to be a lot of people who aren't going to like it, because it's a mountain they can't climb. And they're not *jerks*. They're just not into that. And they don't *have* to be into it. There's other things that they can see. If you *can* climb that mountain, then I'm going to give you something to climb.

GF: *Conventional notions of morality are made complicated in your films. You give your characters a license to kill.*

QT: I'm not trying to preach any kind of morals or get any kind of message across, but for all the wildness that happens in my movies, I think that they usually lead to a moral conclusion. For example, I find what passes between Mr White and Mr Orange at the end of

Reservoir Dogs very moving and profound in its morality and its human interaction.

GF: *Why do you think pop culture, comics, and movies themselves proliferate in your scripts?*

QT: I guess it just comes from me, from what I find fascinating. If I have an interesting take on it, it's not that I'm necessarily lacing it with irony or showing it to you so you can laugh at it. I'm trying to show the enjoyment of it.

GF: *Junk food, too.*

QT: Cap'n Crunch cereal or whatever! It's funny, because I'm actually getting on a more nutritious diet myself. I started writing down this list of bad fast-food restaurants I'd go to to eat a bunch of stuff that I really didn't want to eat. I'm looking at it right now in my apartment and it says, 'Stay away until you absolutely have to go there. Then enjoy it. But don't get used to it.' Then there's a list that says, 'Hanging out with Scott, Roger, and this group of guys!'

GF: *Scott and Roger being the prototypes for the TV crew guys with those names in* Natural Born Killers?

QT: Yeah. And then underneath it says, 'I want to still do that, but I must not do it frequently, and cut down in other areas, so I can still have fun with those guys.' And then another bad place: 'The kitchen at the office' – Cokes and cookies and stuff like that; stay away from there. Empty calories.

GF: *Do you see yourself writing scripts in a more classical style, perhaps less charged with pop-cultural references, and perhaps less frenetic. A period film?*

QT: I don't necessarily want to make anything less frenetic. Not right now. I'll give you an example. L. M. Kit Carson let me read his script for *The Moviegoer*, and indicated that it would be cool by him if I wanted to direct it. I read it and I liked it a lot, but I told him, 'I'm not mature enough to make this movie right now.' Not that the work I'm doing is immature, but I'm still on my own road. Eventually, I'll get off it and want to go in a different direction, or do somebody else's work.

GF: *What has changed about your writing since you began?*

QT: I think it's more sophisticated. I am not chasing it as much. I know the effects I'm after, and I eventually get them. I trust myself more that it will all work out – just keep the characters talking to each other and they'll find the way. After you've done it a few times, you fly blind for a little while, not knowing how you're going to wrap a script up, and then at the last minute something really cool happens. Constantly, what happens in my scripts is that the characters will do something that just blows me away. With regard to the torture scene in *Reservoir Dogs*, I try to explain to people that I didn't sit down and say, 'OK, I'm gonna write this really bitchin' torture scene.' When Mr Blonde reached into his boot and pulled out a straight razor, I didn't know he had a straight razor in his boot. I was surprised. That happens all the time when I'm writing. I equate it to acting. If you're improvising, all of a sudden you say or do something that puts this charge into a scene. That's what it's like writing. The other thing I've learned through acting is that whatever's affecting you that day needs to find a way to be filtered into the work that you're doing. Because if it doesn't, you're denying it.

Basically, I don't come up with any new ideas. I have a stockpile of ideas in my head that goes back five or six years, and when it comes time to write another script or to think about what I want to do next as a writer, I flip through them and find the right one. They're incubating. I'll come up with one of them and say, 'OK, it's not this one's time yet. Let it just sit here and get a little better. Let's do this one instead.' I want to do them all eventually; I know I never will.

GF: *Do your stories come fully formed?*

QT: I always start with scenes I know I am going to put in and scenes from scripts I never finish. Every script I have written has at least twenty pages that are taken from other things I've done. I had the idea for *Pulp Fiction* a long time ago and then I came up with the idea of how to do it in the editing room when we were cutting *Reservoir Dogs*. I thought about it and thought about it, way past the point I normally do. Normally when I can't think about anything else but the script, then I write it. I couldn't do it while I was in the lab but I finally moved to Amsterdam for a couple of months and started writing *Pulp Fiction* there. After thinking about it for six or seven months straight, suddenly what I was writing was completely different. Even though the movie takes place in Los Angeles, I was taking in all this weird being-in-Europe-for-the-first-time stuff and that was finding its way into the script. So some genre story that I'd had for five years started becoming very personal as I wrote it. That's the only way I know how to make the work any good – make it personal.

GF: *How many drafts will you do before you hand it in?*

QT: When I hand in the first draft of a script, it's probably my third draft of it. That's why I'm pretty comfortable with it and can say, 'If you don't like it, then you don't want to do it, because this is what I'm going to do.'

GF: *Do you revise as you proceed, or do you go back and redo the whole thing?*

QT: I revise scenes as I go along, minimally. Usually, I'm just trying to keep going on it.

GF: *Do you write overnight?*

QT: I write into the night.

GF: *On a word processor?*

QT: No, I don't know how to type properly. When I know I'm going to do a script, I'll go to the stationery store and buy a notebook with eighty or a hundred pages in it, where you rip the pages out of the ring file, and I'll say, 'OK, this is the notebook I'm going to write *Pulp Fiction* or whatever in.' I also buy three red felt pens and three black felt pens. I make this big ritual out of it. It's just psychology. I always say that you can't write poetry on a computer, but I can take this notebook places, I can write in restaurants, I can write in friends' houses, I can write standing up, I can write lying down in my bed – I can write everywhere. It never looks like a script; it always looks like Richard Ramirez's diary, the diary of a madman. When I get to my last stage, which is the typing stage, it starts looking like a script for the first time. Then I start making dialogue cuts and fixing up things that didn't work before.

GF: *Do you enjoy the process?*

QT: I usually think it's going to be horrible, but I always have a great time.

GF: *Does it pour out?*

QT: If it doesn't, then I just don't do it that day. If I can't get the characters talking, then I ain't gonna do it. If it's *me* making the characters talk to each other, then that's phoney baloney. It becomes exciting when a character says something and I'm like, 'Wow, he said this? I didn't know that he had a wife or I didn't know he felt like that!'

GF: *So it's a process of discovering what's locked away inside there?*

QT: Very much so. That's why I could *never* do a script treatment where you take the story from beginning to end. I'm not that kind of a writer. There's questions I don't want to answer until I get to writing.

(Abridged from a longer interview that appeared in *Projections 3*)

Reservoir Dogs

RESERVOIR DOGS was first shown at the 1992 Cannes Film Festival. The cast includes:

MR WHITE (Larry)	Harvey Keitel
MR ORANGE (Freddy)	Tim Roth
MR BLONDE (Vic)	Michael Madsen
NICE GUY EDDIE	Chris Penn
MR PINK	Steve Buscemi
JOE CABOT	Lawrence Tierney
HOLDAWAY	Randy Brooks
MARVIN NASH	Kirk Baltz
MR BLUE	Eddie Bunker
MR BROWN	Quentin Tarantino
TEDDY	Michael Sottile
SHOT COP	Robert Ruth
YOUNG COP	Lawrence Bender

Casting by	Ronnie Yeskel
Music Supervisor	Karyn Rachtman
Costume Designer	Betsy Heimann
Production Designer	David Wasco
Editor	Sally Menks
Director of Photography	Andrzej Sekula
Executive Producers	Richard N. Gladstein
	Ronna B. Wallace
	Monte Hellman
Co-Producer	Harvey Keitel
Producer	Lawrence Bender
Written and Directed by	Quentin Tarantino

INT. UNCLE BOB'S PANCAKE HOUSE – MORNING

Eight men dressed in BLACK SUITS, sit around a table at a breakfast café. They are Mr White, Mr Pink, Mr Blue, Mr Blonde, Mr Orange, Mr Brown, Nice Guy Eddie Cabot, and the big boss, Joe Cabot. Most are finished eating and are enjoying coffee and conversation. Joe flips through a small address book. Mr Brown is telling a long and involved story about Madonna.

MR BROWN

'Like a Virgin' is all about a girl who digs a guy with a big dick. The whole song is a metaphor for big dicks.

MR BLONDE

No, it's not. It's about a girl who is very vulnerable and she's been fucked over a few times. Then she meets some guy who's really sensitive –

MR BROWN

– Whoa . . . whoa . . . time out, Greenbay. Tell that bullshit to the tourists.

JOE
(*looking through his address book*)

Toby . . . who the fuck is Toby? Toby . . . Toby . . . think . . . think . . . think . . .

MR BROWN

It's not about a nice girl who meets a sensitive boy. Now granted that's what 'True Blue' is about, no argument about that.

MR ORANGE

Which one is 'True Blue?'

NICE GUY EDDIE

You don't remember 'True Blue'? That was a big ass hit for Madonna. Shit, I don't even follow this Tops in Pops shit, and I've at least heard of 'True Blue'.

MR ORANGE

Look, asshole, I didn't say I ain't heard of it. All I asked was how does it go? Excuse me for not being the world's biggest Madonna fan.

3

MR WHITE

I hate Madonna.

MR BLUE

I like her early stuff. You know, 'Lucky Star', 'Borderline' – but once she got into her 'Papa Don't Preach' phase, I don't know, I tuned out.

MR BROWN

Hey, fuck all that, I'm making a point here. You're gonna make me lose my train of thought.

JOE

Oh fuck, Toby's that little china girl.

MR WHITE

What's that?

JOE

I found this old address book in a jacket I ain't worn in a coon's age. Toby what? What the fuck was her last name?

MR BROWN

Where was I?

MR PINK

You said 'True Blue' was about a nice girl who finds a sensitive fella. But 'Like a Virgin' was a metaphor for big dicks.

MR BROWN

Let me tell ya what 'Like a Virgin''s about. It's about some cooze who's a regular fuck machine. I mean all the time, morning, day, night, afternoon, dick, dick, dick, dick, dick, dick, dick, dick, dick, dick, dick.

MR BLUE

How many dicks was that?

MR PINK

A lot.

MR BROWN

Then one day she meet a John Holmes motherfucker, and it's like, whoa baby. This mother fucker's like Charles Bronson in 'The Great Escape'. He's diggin' tunnels. Now she's gettin' this serious

4

dick action, she's feelin' something she ain't felt since forever. Pain.

JOE

Chew? Toby Chew? No.

MR BROWN

It hurts. It hurts her. It shouldn't hurt. Her pussy should be Bubble-Yum by now. But when this cat fucks her, it hurts. It hurts like the first time. The pain is reminding a fuck machine what it was like to be a virgin. Hence, 'Like a Virgin'.

The fellas crack up.

JOE

Wong?

MR BROWN

Fuck you, wrong. I'm right! What the fuck do you know about it anyway? You're still listening to Jerry-fucking-Vale records.

JOE

Not wrong, dumb ass, Wong! You know, like the Chinese name?

Mr White snatches the address book from Joe's hand. They fight, but they're not really mad at each other.

MR WHITE

Give me this fuckin' thing.

JOE

What the fuck do you think you're doin'? Give me my book back!

MR WHITE

I'm sick of fuckin' hearin' it; Joe, I'll give it back when we leave.

JOE

Whaddaya mean, give it to me when we leave, give it back now.

MR WHITE

For the past fifteen minutes now, you've just been droning on with names. 'Toby . . . Toby . . . Toby . . . Toby Wong . . . Toby Wong . . . Toby Chung . . . fuckin' Charlie Chan.' I got Madonna's big dick outta my right ear, and Toby Jap I-don't-know-what, outta my left.

JOE

What do you care?

MR WHITE

When you're as annoying as hell, I care a lot.

JOE

Give me my book.

MR WHITE

You gonna put it away?

JOE

I'm gonna do whatever I wanna do with it.

MR WHITE

Well, then, I'm afraid I'm gonna have to keep it.

MR BLONDE

Joe, you want me to shoot him for you?

MR WHITE

Shit, you shoot me in a dream, you better wake up and apologize.

NICE GUY EDDIE

Have you guys been listening to K-Billy's super sounds of the seventies weekend?

MR PINK

Yeah, it's fuckin' great, isn't it?

NICE GUY EDDIE

Can you believe the songs they been playin'?

MR PINK

You know what I heard the other day? 'Heartbeat – It's Lovebeat' by little Tony DeFranco and the DeFranco Family. I haven't heard that since I was in fifth fuckin' grade.

NICE GUY EDDIE

When I was coming down here, I was playin' it. And 'The Night the Lights Went Out in Georgia' came on. Now I ain't heard that song since it was big, but when it was big I heard it a million-trillion times. I'm listening to it this morning, and this was the

first time I ever realized that the lady singing the song, was the one
who killed Andy.

MR BROWN
You didn't know Vicki Lawrence killed the guy?

NICE GUY EDDIE
I thought the cheatin' wife shot Andy.

MR BLONDE
They say it in the song.

NICE GUY EDDIE
I know, I heard it. I musta zoned out whenever that part came on
before. I thought when she said that little sister stuff, she was
talkin' about her sister-in-law, the cheatin' wife.

JOE
No, she did it. She killed the cheatin' wife, too.

MR WHITE
Who gives a damn?

*The table laughs. The Waitress comes over to the table. She has the
check, and a pot of coffee.*

WAITRESS
Can I get anybody more coffee?

JOE
No, we're gonna be hittin' it. I'll take care of the check.

She hands the bill to him.

WAITRESS
Here ya go. Please pay at the register, if you wouldn't mind.

JOE
Sure thing.

WAITRESS
You guys have a wonderful day.

They all mutter equivalents. She exits and Joe stands up.

JOE
I'll take care of this, you guys leave the tip.

(to Mr White)
And when I come back, I want my book back.

MR WHITE

Sorry, it's my book now.

JOE

Blue, shoot this piece of shit, will ya?

Mr Blue shoots Mr White with his finger. Mr White acts shot. Joe exits.

NICE GUY EDDIE

Okay, everybody cough up green for the little lady.

Everybody whips out a buck, and throws it on the table. Everybody, that is, except Mr Pink.

C'mon, throw in a buck.

MR PINK

Uh-uh. I don't tip.

NICE GUY EDDIE

Whaddaya mean, you don't tip?

MR PINK

I don't believe in it.

NICE GUY EDDIE

You don't believe in tipping?

MR BROWN
(laughing)
I love this guy, he's a madman, this guy.

MR BLONDE

Do you have any idea what these ladies make? They make shit.

MR PINK

Don't give me that. She don't make enough money, she can quit.

Everybody laughs.

NICE GUY EDDIE

I don't even know a Jew who'd have the balls to say that. So let's get this straight. You never ever tip?

8

                    MR PINK
I don't tip because society says I gotta. I tip when somebody
deserves a tip. When somebody really puts forth an effort, they
deserve a little something extra. But this tipping automatically,
that shit's for the birds. As far as I'm concerned, they're just doin'
their job.

                    MR BLUE
Our girl was nice.

                    MR PINK
Our girl was okay. She didn't do anything special.

                    MR BLUE
What's something special, take ya in the kitchen and suck your
dick?

They all laugh.

                 NICE GUY EDDIE
I'd go over twelve percent for that.

                    MR PINK
Look, I ordered coffee. Now we've been here a long fuckin' time,
and she's only filled my cup three times. When I order coffee, I
want it filled six times.

                    MR BLONDE
What if it's too busy?

                    MR PINK
The words 'too busy' shouldn't be in a waitress's vocabulary.

                 NICE GUY EDDIE
Excuse me, Mr Pink, but the last thing you need is another cup of
coffee.

They all laugh.

                    MR PINK
These ladies aren't starvin' to death. They make minimum wage.
When I worked for minimum wage, I wasn't lucky enough to have
a job that society deemed tipworthy.

NICE GUY EDDIE

Ahh, now we're getting down to it. It's not just that he's a cheap bastard –

MR ORANGE

– It is that too –

NICE GUY EDDIE

– It is that too. But it's also he couldn't get a waiter job. You talk like a pissed-off dishwasher: 'Fuck those cunts and their fucking tips.'

MR BLONDE

So you don't care that they're counting on your tip to live?

Mr Pink rubs two of his fingers together.

MR PINK

Do you know what this is? It's the world's smallest violin, playing just for the waitresses.

MR WHITE

You don't have any idea what you're talking about. These people bust their ass. This is a hard job.

MR PINK

So's working at McDonalds, but you don't feel the need to tip them. They're servin' ya food, you should tip 'em. But no, society says tip these guys over here, but not those guys over there. That's bullshit.

MR BLUE

They work harder than the kids at McDonalds.

MR PINK

Oh yeah, I don't see them cleaning fryers.

MR BLUE

These ladies are taxed on the tips they make. When you stiff 'em, you cost them money.

MR WHITE

Waitressing is the number one occupation for female non-college graduates in this country. It's the one job basically any woman can get, and make a living on. The reason is because of tips.

MR PINK
Fuck all that.

They all laugh.

                              MR PINK
Hey, I'm very sorry that the government taxes their tips. That's
fucked up. But that ain't my fault. It would appear that waitresses
are just one of the many groups the government fucks in the ass on
a regular basis. You show me a paper says the government
shouldn't do that, I'll sign it. Put it to a vote, I'll vote for it. But
what I won't do is play ball. And this non-college bullshit you're
telling me, I got two words for that: 'Learn to fuckin' type.'
'Cause if you're expecting me to help out with the rent, you're in
for a big fuckin' surprise.

                             MR ORANGE
He's convinced me. Give me my dollar back.

Everybody laughs. Joe comes back to the table.

                                JOE
Okay ramblers, let's get to rambling. Wait a minute, who didn't
throw in?

                             MR ORANGE
Mr Pink.

                                JOE
                          (*to Mr Orange*)
Mr Pink?

                           (*to Mr Pink*)
Why?

                             MR ORANGE
He don't tip.

                                JOE
                          (*to Mr Orange*)
He don't tip?

                           (*to Mr Pink*)
You don't tip? Why?

                                 11

MR ORANGE

He don't believe in it.

JOE
(*to Mr Orange*)

He don't believe in it?

(*to Mr Pink*)

You don't believe in it?

MR ORANGE

Nope.

JOE
(*to Mr Orange*)

Shut up!

(*to Mr Pink*)

Cough up the buck, ya cheap bastard, I paid for your goddam breakfast.

MR PINK

Because you paid for the breakfast, I'm gonna tip. Normally I wouldn't.

JOE

Whatever. Just throw in your dollar, and let's move.
(*to Mr White*)
See what I'm dealing with here. Infants. I'm fuckin' dealin' with infants.

The eight men get up to leave. Mr White's waist is in the foreground. As he buttons his coat, for a second we see he's carrying a gun. They exit Uncle Bob's Pancake House, talking amongst themselves.

★[TITLE CARD:

'ONE OF THESE MEN IS A COP.'

Then underneath it:

'AND BY THE END, ALL BUT ONE WILL BE DEAD.']

★ Cut from completed film.

EXT. UNCLE BOB'S PANCAKE HOUSE – DAY

CREDIT SEQUENCE:

When the credit sequence is finished, fade to black.

Over the black we hear the sound of someone screaming in agony.

Under the screaming, we hear the sound of a car hauling ass, through traffic.

Over the screams and the traffic noise, we hear somebody else say:

> SOMEBODY ELSE
> (*off*)
> Just hold on buddy boy.

Somebody stops screaming long enough to say:

> SOMEBODY
> (*off*)
> I'm sorry. I can't believe she killed me. Who would've fuckin' thought that?

CUT TO:

INT. GETAWAY CAR (MOVING) – DAY

The Somebody screaming is Mr Orange. He lies in the backseat. He's been shot in the stomach. Blood covers both him and the backseat.

Mr White is the Somebody Else. He's behind the wheel of the getaway car. He's easily doing 80 mph, dodging in and out of traffic. Though he's driving for his life, he keeps talking to his wounded passenger in the backseat.

They are the only two in the car.

> MR WHITE
> Hey, just cancel that shit right now! You're hurt. You're hurt really fucking bad, but you ain't dying.

> MR ORANGE
> (*crying*)
> All this blood is scaring the shit outta me. I'm gonna die, I know it.

MR WHITE

Oh excuse me, I didn't realize you had a degree in medicine. Are
you a doctor? Are you a doctor? Answer me please, are you a
doctor?

MR ORANGE

No, I'm not!

MR WHITE

Ahhhh, so you admit you don't know what you're talking about.
So if you're through giving me your amateur opinion, lie back and
listen to the news. I'm taking you back to the rendezvous, Joe's
gonna get you a doctor, the doctor's gonna fix you up, and you're
gonna be okay. Now say it: you're gonna be okay. *Say it*: you're
gonna be okay!

*Mr Orange doesn't respond. Mr White starts pounding on the steering
wheel.*

MR WHITE

Say-the-goddam-words: you're gonna be okay!

MR ORANGE

I'm okay.

MR WHITE
(*softly*)

Correct.

INT. WAREHOUSE – DAY

*The Camera does a 360 around an empty warehouse. Then the door
swings open, and Mr White carries the bloody body of Mr Orange inside.*

Mr Orange still is moaning loudly from his bullet hit.

Mr White lays him down upon a mattress on the floor.

MR WHITE

Just hold on, buddy boy. Hold on, and wait for Joe. I can't do
anything for you, but when Joe gets here, which should be any
time now, he'll be able to help you. We're just gonna sit here, and
wait for Joe. Who are we waiting for?

MR ORANGE

Joe.

MR WHITE

Bet your sweet ass we are.

MR ORANGE

Larry, I'm so scared, would you please hold me.

Mr White very gently embraces the bloody Mr Orange. Cradling the young man, Mr White whispers to him.

MR WHITE
(whispering)

Go ahead and be scared, you've been brave enough for one day. I want you to just relax now. You're not gonna die, you're gonna be fine. When Joe gets here, he'll make ya a hundred percent again.

Mr White lays Mr Orange back down. He's still holding his hand. Mr Orange looks up at his friend.

MR ORANGE

Look, I don't wanna be a fly in the ointment, but if help doesn't come soon, I gotta see a doctor. I don't give a fuck about jail, I just don't wanna die.

MR WHITE

You're not gonna fucking die, all right?

MR ORANGE

I wasn't born yesterday. I'm hurt, and I'm hurt bad.

MR WHITE

It's not good . . .

MR ORANGE

Hey, bless your heart for what you're trying to do. I was panicking for a moment, but I've got my senses back now. The situation is, I'm shot in the belly. And without medical attention, I'm gonna die.

MR WHITE

I can't take you to a hospital.

16

MR ORANGE

Fuck jail! I don't give a shit about jail. But I can't die. You don't
have to take me in. Just drive me up to the front, drop me on the
sidewalk. I'll take care of myself. I won't tell them anything. I
swear to fucking God, I won't tell 'em anything. Look in my eyes,
look right in my eyes.

(*Mr White does*)

I-won't-tell-them-anything. You'll be safe.

MR WHITE

Lie back down, and try to –

MR ORANGE

I'm going to die! I need a doctor! I'm begging you, take me to a
doctor.

MR WHITE

Listen to me, kid. You ain't gonna die! Along with the kneecap,
the gut is the most painful area a guy can get shot in.

MR ORANGE

No shit.

MR WHITE

But it takes a long time to die from it. I'm talkin' days. You'll wish
you were dead, but it takes days to die from your wound. Time is
on your side. When Joe gets here, he'll have a doctor patch you up
in nothin' flat. You know how Joe operates. He's got MD's in his
back pocket. Just bite the fuckin' bullet and wait for Joe to get
here.

Mr Orange lays his head back. He quietly mutters to himself:

MR ORANGE

Take me to a doctor, take me to a doctor, please.

Suddenly, the warehouse door bursts open and Mr Pink steps inside.

MR PINK

Was that a fucking set-up or what?

Mr Pink sees Mr Orange on the floor, shot and bloody.

MR PINK

Oh fuck, Orange got tagged.

Throughout this scene, we hear Mr Orange moaning.

MR WHITE

Gut shot.

MR PINK

Oh that's just fucking great! Where's Brown?

MR WHITE

Dead.

MR PINK

Goddam, goddam! How did he die?

MR WHITE

How the fuck do you think? The cops shot him.

MR PINK

Oh this is bad, this is so bad.
                    (*referring to Mr Orange*)
Is it bad?

MR WHITE

As opposed to good?

MR PINK

This is so fucked up. Somebody fucked us big time.

MR WHITE

You really think we were set up?

MR PINK

You even doubt it? I don't think we got set up, I know we got set up!
I mean really, seriously, where did all those cops come from, huh?
One minute they're not there, the next minute they're there. I
didn't hear any sirens. The alarm went off, okay. Okay, when an
alarm goes off, you got an average of four minutes response time.
Unless a patrol car is cruising that street, at that particular moment,
you got four minutes before they can realistically respond. In one
minute there were seventeen blue boys out there. All loaded for
bear, all knowing exactly what the fuck they were doing, and they
were all just there! Remember that second wave that showed up in
the cars? Those were the ones responding to the alarm, but those
other motherfuckers were already there, they were waiting for us.
                    (*pause*)
You haven't thought about this?

MR WHITE

I haven't had a chance to think. First I was just trying to get the fuck
outta there. And after we got away, I've just been dealin' with him.

MR PINK

Well, you better start thinking about it. 'Cause I, sure as fuck, am
thinking about it. In fact, that's all I'm thinking about. I came this
close to just driving off. Whoever set us up, knows about this place.
There could've been cops sitting here waiting for me. For all we
know, there's cops, driving fast, on their way here now.

MR WHITE

Let's go in the other room.

*The camera creeps along a wall, coming to a corner. We move past it, and
see down a hall.*

INT. BATHROOM HALLWAY — DAY

At the end of the hall is a bathroom. The bathroom door is partially closed, restricting our view. Mr Pink is obscured, but Mr White is in view.

MR PINK
(off)

What the fuck am I doing here? I felt funny about this job right off. As soon as I felt it I should have said 'No thank you', and walked. But I never fucking listen. Every time I ever got burned buying weed, I always knew the guy wasn't right. I just felt it. But I wanted to believe him. If he's not lyin' to me, and it really is Thai stick, then whoa baby. But it's never Thai stick. And I always said if I felt that way about a job, I'd walk. And I did, and I didn't, because of fuckin' money!

MR WHITE

What's done is done, I need you cool. Are you cool?

MR PINK

I'm cool.

MR WHITE

Splash some water on your face. Take a breather.

We hear the sink running, and Mr Pink splashing water on his face. He takes out his gun and lays it on the counter.

I'm gonna get me my smokes.

Mr White opens the bathroom door, walks down the hall, and out of frame. We see Mr Pink, his back turned towards us, bent over the sink. Then he grabs a towel, and dries his face. Mr White enters frame with a pack of Chesterfields in his hand.

Want a smoke?

MR PINK

Why not?

The two men light up.

MR WHITE

Okay, let's go through what happened. We're in the place, everything's going fine. Then the alarm gets tripped. I turn around

and all these cops are outside. You're right, it was like, bam! I blink my eyes and they're there. Everybody starts going apeshit. Then Mr Blonde starts shootin' all the –

MR PINK

– That's not correct.

MR WHITE

What's wrong with it?

MR PINK

The cops didn't show up after the alarm went off. They didn't show till after Mr Blonde started shooting everyone.

MR WHITE

As soon as I heard the alarm, I saw the cops.

MR PINK

I'm telling ya, it wasn't that soon. They didn't let their presence be known until after Mr Blonde went off. I'm not sayin' they weren't there, I'm sayin' they were there. But they didn't move in till Mr Blonde became a madman. That's how I know we were set up. You can see that, can't you, Mr White?

MR WHITE
Look, enough of this 'Mr White' shit –

MR PINK
– Don't tell me your name, I don't want to know! I sure as hell
ain't gonna tell ya mine.

MR WHITE
You're right, this is bad.
(pause)
How did you get out?

MR PINK
Shot my way out. Everybody was shooting, so I just blasted my
way outta there.

CUT TO:

EXT. CROWDED CITY STREET – DAY

*Mr Pink is hauling ass down a busy city sidewalk. He has a canvas bag
with a shoulder strap in one hand, and a .357 Magnum in the other. If
any bystanders get in his way, he just knocks them down. We dolly at the
same speed, right alongside of him.*

*Four Policemen are running after Mr Pink. Three are running together,
and one fat one is lagging a few paces behind. We dolly with them.*

In his mad dash Mr Pink runs into the street, and is hit by a moving car.

He's thrown up on the hood, cracking the windshield, and rolling off.

INT. CAR (STOPPED) – DAY

*The camera is in the backseat. A shocked woman is the car's driver. Mr
Pink pulls himself up from the hood, shakes himself off, and points his
magnum at the driver.*

MR PINK
Get outta the car! Get the fuck outta the car!

The Shocked Woman starts screaming.

Mr Pink tries to open the driver's side door, but it's locked.

                              MR PINK
Open the fucking door!

EXTREME CU – DRIVER'S SIDE WINDOW

Mr Pink SMASHES it in our face.

EXT. STREET – DAY

Dolly with Cops coming up fast.

Mr Pink drags the Shocked Woman out of the car.

The Cops reach the corner, guns aimed.

Using the car as a shield, Mr Pink fires three shots at the Cops.

Everybody hits the ground, or scatters.

Cops fire. Mr Pink unloads his gun.

Fat Cop is shot in his pot belly, falls back in the arms of a Young Cop. The Fat Cop screams in pain, the Young Cop screams in anguish.

Mr Pink hops in the car. Cops fire.

INT. CAR (MOVING) – DAY

Camera in the backseat, Mr Pink floors it. Speeding down the street, with the Cops firing after him.

EXT. STREET – DAY

The Young Cop takes off running and firing after the getaway car. It's no use. Mr Pink leaves him in the dust.

   BACK TO:

INT. BATHROOM – DAY

Mr Pink and Mr White still talking in the bathroom.

                              MR PINK
Tagged a couple of cops. Did you kill anybody?

MR WHITE

A few cops.

MR PINK

No real people?

MR WHITE

Uh-uh, just cops.

MR PINK

Could you believe Mr Blonde?

MR WHITE

That was one of the most insane fucking things I've ever seen.
Why the fuck would Joe hire somebody like that?

MR PINK

I don't wanna kill anybody. But if I gotta get out that door, and
you're standing in my way, one way or the other, you're gettin'
outta my way.

MR WHITE

That's the way I look at it. A choice between doin' ten years, and
takin' out some stupid motherfucker, ain't no choice at all. But I
ain't no madman either. What the fuck was Joe thinkin'? You
can't work with a guy like that. We're awful goddamn lucky he
didn't tag us, when he shot up the place. I came this fucking
close –
     (holds up two fingers and makes a tiny space between them)
– to taking his ass out myself.

MR PINK

Everybody panics. When things get tense, everybody panics.
Everybody. I don't care what your name is, you can't help it. It's
human nature. But ya panic on the inside. Ya panic in your head.
Ya give yourself a couple a seconds of panic, then you get a grip
and deal with the situation. What you don't do, is shoot up the
place and kill everybody.

MR WHITE

What you're supposed to do is act like a fuckin' professional. A
psychopath is not a professional. You can't work with a
psychopath, 'cause ya don't know what those sick assholes are

gonna do next. I mean, Jesus Christ, how old do you think that black girl was? Twenty, maybe twenty-one?

MR PINK
Did ya see what happened to anybody else?

MR WHITE
Me and Mr Orange jumped in the car and Mr Brown floored it. After that, I don't know what went down.

MR PINK
At that point it became every man for himself. As far as Mr Blonde or Mr Blue are concerned, I ain't got the foggiest. Once I got out, I never looked back.

MR WHITE
What do you think?

MR PINK
What do I think? I think the cops caught them, or killed 'em.

MR WHITE
Not even a chance they punched through? You found a hole.

MR PINK
Yeah, and that was a fucking miracle. But if they did get away, where the fuck are they?

MR WHITE
You don't think it's possible, one of them got a hold of the diamonds and pulled a –

MR PINK
Nope.

MR WHITE
How can you be so sure?

MR PINK
I got the diamonds.

MR WHITE
Where?

MR PINK
I stashed 'em. You wanna go with me and get 'em? Sure, we can

26

go right now, we can leave this second. I think we should have our fuckin' heads examined for waiting around here.

MR WHITE
That was the plan, we meet here.

MR PINK
Then where is everybody? I say the plan became null and void once we found out we got a rat in the house. We ain't got the slightest fuckin' idea what happened to Mr Blonde or Mr Blue. They could both be dead or arrested. They could be sweatin' 'em, down at the station house right now. Yeah they don't know our names, but they can sing about this place.

MR WHITE
I swear to god I'm fuckin' jinxed.

MR PINK
What?

MR WHITE
Two jobs back, it was a four-man job, we discovered one of the team was an undercover cop.

MR PINK
No shit?

MR WHITE
Thank God, we discovered in time. We hadda forget the whole fuckin' thing. Just walked away from it.

MR PINK
So who's the rat this time? Mr Blue? Mr Blonde? Joe? It's Joe's show, he set this whole thing up. Maybe he set it up to set it up.

MR WHITE
I don't buy it. Me and Joe go back a long time. I can tell ya straight up, Joe definitely didn't have anything to do with this bullshit.

MR PINK
Oh, you and Joe go back a long time. I known Joe since I was a kid. But me saying Joe definitely couldn't have done it is ridiculous. I can say I definitely didn't do it, 'cause I know what I

did or didn't do. But I can't definitely say that about anybody else, 'cause I don't definitely know. For all I know, you're the rat.

MR WHITE

For all I know, you're the rat.

MR PINK

Now you're using your head. For all we know, he's the rat.

MR WHITE

That kid in there is dying from a fuckin' bullet that I saw him take. So don't be calling him a rat.

MR PINK

Look, asshole, I'm right! Somebody's a fuckin' rat. How many times do I hafta say it before it sinks in your skull.

The talking stops. The two men just stare at each other. Mr Pink breaks the silence.

MR PINK

I gotta take a squint, where's the commode in this dungeon?

MR WHITE

Go down the hall, turn left, up those stairs, then turn right.

Mr Pink exits frame, leaving Mr White alone.

CUT TO:

TITLE CARD:

'MR WHITE'

EMPTY FRAME

In the background we see what looks like an office set up.

VOICE

How's Alabama?

MR WHITE

Alabama? I haven't seen Bama over a year and a half.

VOICE

I thought you two were a team.

MR WHITE

We were for a little while. Did about four jobs together. Then decided to call it quits. You push it long enough that woman man thing gets in your way after a while.

We now cut to see Joe behind his desk.

JOE

What's she doin' now?

MR WHITE

She hooked up with Fred McGar, they've done a coupla jobs together. Helluva woman. Good little thief. *[I heard tell you tied the knot with a gorgeous gal.

JOE
(*laughs*)

Tammy's a looker all right.

MR WHITE

I heard she's from Arkansas.

JOE

Tennessee. Knoxville, Tennessee. She used to be a regular on *Hee-Haw*. You know that country show with all those fuckin' hicks.

MR WHITE

I know what *Hee-Haw* is.
(*pause*)
So why did ya marry her?

JOE

I love her. Pretty silly, an old fart like me, huh?

MR WHITE

It's kinda silly. It's kinda cute, too.

JOE

You know what's really silly? She loves me back. I know you won't believe that, but I don't give a damn, because I know she does. You know what she's got me doin', Larry, readin' books. She'll read somethin', come to me and say, 'Joe' – in that funny accent she has, sounds like Li'l Abner – 'Joe, I just read this book

* Cut from completed film.

30

and it's really good. And I want you to read it, 'cause I want to talk
with you about it.' And if I know what's good for me, I better read
it. I'm turnin' into a regular bookworm. I always got a paperback
with me.

Joe opens his desk and throws a dogeared paperback of The Bell Jar *on the desk. Mr White looks at it.*

JOE

Ya ever read it?

Mr White shakes his head.

Tammy loves that Sylvia Plath. I ain't so sure, myself. She killed herself, ya know.

MR WHITE

Tammy?

JOE

No, asshole, Plath. The woman who wrote the goddamn book. Look, I know everybody thinks I'm a chump, but they're wrong and I'm right. I know how she feels about me, and how she makes me feel when I'm with her. And that's good enough for me.

MR WHITE

Plath?

Joe gives White a hard look. Mr White laughs.

What's hard to believe? You're a lovable guy. In fact, Joe, I'd go so far as to describe you as a catch.

JOE
(*laughing*)

Keep needling me, Weisenheimer, and you're gonna meet Mr Boot.

Mr White walks over to the side of the desk.

MR WHITE

We've met. And Mr Butt wants to stay far away.] So, explain the telegram.

JOE

Five-man job. Bustin' in and bustin' out of a diamond wholesaler's.

MR WHITE

Can you move the ice afterwards? I don't know nobody who can move ice.

                            JOE
Not a problem, got guys waitin' for it. But what happened to
Marcellus Spivey? Didn't he always move your ice?

                         MR WHITE
He's doin' twenty years in Susanville.

                            JOE
What for?

                         MR WHITE
Bad luck. What's the exposure like?

                            JOE
Two minutes, tops. It's a tough two minutes. It's daylight, during
business hours, dealing with a crowd. But you'll have the guys to
deal with the crowd.

                         MR WHITE
How many employees?

                            JOE
Around twenty. Security pretty lax. They almost always just deal
in boxes. Rough uncut stones they get from the syndicate. On a
certain day this wholesaler's gettin' a big shipment of polished
stones from Israel. They're like a way station. They're gonna get
picked up the next day and sent to Vermont.

                         MR WHITE
No they're not.

The men share a laugh.

What's the cut, poppa?

                            JOE
Juicy, junior, real juicy.

FADE TO BLACK

BACK TO THE GARAGE

*We follow Mr Pink, handheld, back through the rooms and hallways to
the garage. We follow behind him up to Mr White, who's standing over
Mr Orange.*

MR PINK

So, I don't know about you, but me – I'm gonna split, check into a motel and lay low for a few days.

As he gets closer he sees Mr Orange is out. He runs over to them.

Holy shit, did he fuckin' die on us?

Mr White doesn't respond.

So, is he dead or what?

MR WHITE

He ain't dead.

MR PINK

So what is it?

MR WHITE

I think he's just passed out.

MR PINK

He scared the fuckin' shit outta me. I thought he was dead fer sure.

Mr White stands up and walks over to a table.

MR WHITE

He will be dead fer sure, if we don't get him to a hospital.

MR PINK

We can't take him to a hospital.

MR WHITE

Without medical attention, this man won't live through the night. That bullet in his belly is my fault. Now while that might not mean jack shit to you, it means a helluva lot to me. And I'm not gonna just sit around and watch him die.

MR PINK

Well, first things first, staying here's goofy. We gotta book up.

MR WHITE

So what do you suggest, we go to a hotel? We got a guy who's shot in the belly, he can't walk, he bleeds like a stuck pig, and when he's awake, he screams in pain.

MR PINK

You gotta idea, spit it out.

MR WHITE

Joe could help him. If we can get in touch with Joe, Joe could get him to a doctor, Joe could get a doctor to come and see him.

During Mr Pink's dialogue, we slowly zoom in to a closeup of Mr White.

MR PINK
(*off*)

Assuming we can trust Joe, how we gonna get in touch with him? He's supposed to be here, but he ain't, which is making me nervous about being here. Even if Joe is on the up and up, he's probably not gonna be that happy with us. Joe planned a robbery, but he's got a blood bath on his hands now. Dead cops, dead robbers, dead civilians . . . Jesus Christ! I tend to doubt he's gonna have a lot of sympathy for our plight. If I was him, I'd try and put as much distance between me and this mess as humanly possible.

MR WHITE

Before you got here, Mr Orange was askin' me to take him to a hospital. Now I don't like turning him over to the cops, but if we don't, he's dead. He begged me to do it. I told him to hold off till Joe got here.

MR PINK
(*off*)

Well Joe ain't gettin' here. We're on our own. Now, I don't know a goddamn body who can help him, so if you know somebody, call 'em.'

MR WHITE

I don't know anybody.

MR PINK
(*off*)

Well, I guess we drop him off at the hospital. Since he don't know nothin' about us, I say it's his decision.

CLOSEUP – MR PINK

> MR WHITE
> (*off*)
> Well, he knows a little about me.

> MR PINK
> You didn't tell him your name, did ya?

> MR WHITE
> (*off*)
> I told him my first name, and where I'm from.

There is a long silence and a blank look from Mr Pink, then he screams:

> MR PINK
> Why?

> MR WHITE
> (*off*)
> I told him where I was from a few days ago. It was just a casual conversation.

> MR PINK
> And what was telling' him your name when you weren't supposed to?

> MR WHITE
> (*off*)
> He asked.

Mr Pink looks at Mr White as if he's retarded.

We had just gotten away from the cops. He just got shot. It was my fuckin' fault he got shot. He's a fuckin' bloody mess – he's screaming. I swear to God, I thought he was gonna die right then and there. I'm tryin' to comfort him, telling him not to worry, he's gonna be okay, I'm gonna take care of him. And he asked me what my name was. I mean, the man was dyin' in my arms. What the fuck was I supposed to tell him, 'Sorry, I can't give out that information, it's against the rules. I don't trust you enough?' Maybe I shoulda, but I couldn't.

MR PINK
Oh, I don't doubt it was quite beautiful –

MR WHITE
(*off*)
Don't fuckin' patronize me.

MR PINK
One question: Do they have a sheet on you, where you told him you're from?

MR WHITE
(*off*)
Of course.

MR PINK
Well that's that, then. I mean, I was worried about mug shot possibilities already. But now he knows: (a) what you look like (b) what your first name is, (c) where you're from and (d) what your speciality is. They ain't gonna hafta show him a helluva lot of pictures for him to pick you out. That's it, right? You didn't tell him anything else that could narrow down the selection?

MR WHITE
(*off*)
If I have to tell you again to back off, me an' you are gonna go round and round.

Mr Pink walks out of the closeup and turns his back on Mr White. Mr White's POV pans over to him.

MR PINK
We ain't taking him to a hospital.

MR WHITE
(*off*)
If we don't, he'll die.

MR PINK
And I'm very sad about that. But some fellas are lucky, and some ain't.

MR WHITE
(*off*)
That fuckin' did it!

38

Mr White's POV charges toward Mr Pink.

Mr Pink turns toward him in time to get punched hard in the mouth.

END OF POV

Mr White and Mr Pink have a very ungraceful and realistic fight. They go at each other like a couple of alley cats.

As Mr White swings and punches, he screams:

> MR WHITE
> You little motherfucker!

Mr Pink yells as he hits:

> MR PINK
> Ya wanna fuck with me?! You wanna fuck with me?! I'll show you who you're fuckin' with!

The two men end up on the floor kicking and scratching. Mr White gets Mr Pink in a headlock.

Mr Pink reaches in his jacket for his gun, and pulls it out. Mr White sees this, immediately lets go of Mr Pink, and goes for his own weapon.

The two men are on the floor, on their knees, with their guns outstretched, aiming at one another.

MR WHITE
You wanna shoot me, you little piece of shit? Take a shot!

Fuck you, White! I didn't create this situation, I'm just dealin'
with it. You're actin' like a first-year fuckin' thief. I'm actin' like a
professional. They get him, they can get you, they get you, they
get closer to me, and that can't happen. And you, you
motherfucker, are lookin' at me like it's my fault. I didn't tell him
my name. I didn't tell him where I was from. I didn't tell him
what I knew better than to tell him. Fuck, fifteen minutes ago,
you almost told me your name. You, buddy, are stuck in a
situation you created. So, if you wanna throw bad looks
somewhere, throw 'em at a mirror.

Mr Pink lowers his gun.

Then from off screen we hear:

VOICE
You kids don't play so rough. Somebody's gonna start crying.

INT. WAREHOUSE – DAY – MEDIUM CLOSEUP ON MR BLONDE

The Voice belongs to the infamous Mr Blonde.

Mr Blonde leans against a pole, drinking a fast-food Coke.

MR PINK
Mr Blonde! You okay? We thought you might've gotten caught.
What happened?

Mr Blonde doesn't answer.

He stares at Mr Pink and Mr White, sipping his Coke.

*This is making Pink and White nervous as hell. But Mr Pink tries to talk
through it.*

Really, how did you get away?

Silence from Mr Blonde.

Where's Mr Blue?

Silence.

We were hopin' you two would be together.

Silence.

We were worried the cops got ya.

Silence.

Look, Brown is dead, Orange got it in the belly.

MR WHITE

Enough! You better start talkin' to us, asshole, 'cause we got shit we need to talk about. We're already freaked out, we need you actin' freaky like we need a fuckin' bag on our hip.

Mr Blonde looks at his two partners in crime, then moves towards them.

MR BLONDE

So, talk.

MR WHITE

We think we got a rat in the house.

MR PINK

I guarantee we got a rat in the house.

MR BLONDE

What would ever make you think that?

MR WHITE

Is that supposed to be funny?

MR PINK

We don't think this place is safe.

MR WHITE

This place just ain't secure any more. We're leaving, and you should go with us.

MR BLONDE

Nobody's going anywhere.

Silence takes over the room. Mr Blonde stops moving. After a few beats the silence is broken.

MR WHITE
(*to Mr Pink*)

Piss on this turd, we're outta here.

Mr White turns to leave.

MR BLONDE

Don't take another step, Mr White.

Mr White explodes, raising his gun and charging towards Mr Blonde.

MR WHITE

Fuck you, maniac! It's your fuckin' fault we're in so much trouble.

Mr Blonde calmly sits down. He looks to Mr Pink.

MR BLONDE
(*referring to Mr White*)

What's this guy's problem?

MR WHITE

What's my problem? Yeah, I gotta problem. I gotta big problem with any trigger-happy madman who almost gets me shot!

MR BLONDE

What're you talkin' about?

MR WHITE

That fuckin' shooting spree in the store.

MR BLONDE

Fuck 'em, they set off the alarm, they deserve what they got.

MR WHITE

You almost killed me, asshole! If I had any idea what type of guy you were, I never would've agreed to work with you.

MR BLONDE

You gonna bark all day, little doggie, or are you gonna bite?

MR WHITE

What was that? I'm sorry, I didn't catch it. Would you repeat it?

MR BLONDE
(*calm and slow*)

I said: 'Are you gonna bark all day, doggie, or are you gonna bite.'

MR PINK

Both of you two assholes knock it the fuck off and calm down!

MR WHITE
(*to Mr Blonde*)
So you wanna git bit, huh?

MR PINK
Cut the bullshit, we ain't on a fuckin' playground!
(*pause*)
I don't believe this shit, both of you got ten years on me, and I'm
the only one actin' like a professional. You guys act like a bunch
of fuckin' niggers. You ever work a job with a bunch of niggers?
They're just like you two, always fightin', always sayin' they're
gonna kill one another.

MR WHITE
(*to Mr Pink*)
You said yourself, you thought about takin' him out.

MR PINK
Then. That time has passed. Right now, Mr Blonde is the only
one I completely trust. He's too fuckin' homicidal to be workin'
with the cops.

MR WHITE
You takin' his side?

MR PINK
Fuck sides! What we need is a little solidarity here. Somebody's
stickin' a red hot poker up our asses and we gotta find out whose
hand's on the handle. Now I know I'm no piece of shit . . .
(*referring to Mr White*)
And I'm pretty sure you're a good boy . . .
(*referring to Mr Blonde*)
And I'm fuckin' positive you're on the level. So let's figure out
who's the bad guy.

Mr White calms down and puts his gun away.

MR BLONDE
Well, that was sure exciting.
(*to Mr White*)
You're a big Lee Marvin fan, aren't you? Me too. I don't know
about the rest of you fellas, but my heart's beatin' fast.

> *(pause for a beat)*
Okay, you guys, follow me.

Mr Blonde hops out of his chair and heads for the door.

The other two men just follow him with their eyes.

MR WHITE
Follow you where?

MR BLONDE
Down to my car.

MR WHITE
Why?

MR BLONDE
It's a surprise.

Mr Blonde walks out the door.

EXT. WAREHOUSE — DAY

Three cars are parked out front. Mr Blonde is walking towards the car he drove. Mr White and Mr Pink are walking behind. The camera is handheld following behind them.

MR PINK
We still gotta get out of here.

MR BLONDE
We're gonna sit here and wait.

MR WHITE
For what, the cops?

MR BLONDE
Nice Guy Eddie.

MR PINK
Nice Guy Eddie? What makes you think Nice Guy's anywhere but on a plane half way to Costa Rica?

MR BLONDE
'Cause I just talked to him. He's on his way down here, and nobody's going anywhere till he gets here.

MR WHITE

You talked to Nice Guy Eddie? Why the fuck didn't you say that in the first place?

MR BLONDE

You didn't ask.

MR WHITE

Hardy-fuckin'-har. What did he say?

MR BLONDE

Stay put. Okay, fellas, take a look at the little surprise I brought you.

Mr Blonde opens up the trunk of his car. A handcuffed, uniformed policeman is curled up inside the trunk.

MR BLONDE

Since we gotta wait for Nice Guy anyway, let's talk to our boy in blue here and see if he knows anything about this rat business.

The three crooks share a frightening laugh. We slowly zoom into a close up of the cop.

CUT TO:

TITLE CARD:

'MR BLONDE'

INT. JOE CABOT'S OFFICE – DAY

We're inside the office of Joe Cabot. Joe's on the phone, sitting behind his desk.

JOE
(*into phone*)

Sid, I'm tellin' you don't worry about it. You had a bad couple of months, it happens.

(*pause*)

Sid . . . Stop, you're embarrassing me. I don't need to be told what I already know. When you have bad months, you do what every businessman in the world does, I don't care if he's J. P. Morgan or Irving the tailor. Ya ride it out.

There's a knock on Cabot's office door.

  Come in.

One of Cabot's goons, Teddy, opens the door and steps inside. Cabot covers the receiver with his hand and looks towards the man.

                    TEDDY
  Vic Vega's outside.

                     JOE
  Tell him to come in.

Teddy leaves.

                    (*into phone*)
  Sid, a friend of mine's here. I gotta go.
                    (*pause*)
  Good enough, bye.

He hangs up the phone, stands, and walks around to the front of his desk.

Teddy opens the office door, and Toothpick Vic Vega walks in.

Toothpick Vic Vega is none other than our very own Mr Blonde. Vic is dressed in a long black leather seventies style jacket.

Joe stands in front of his desk with his arms open.

The two men embrace. Teddy leaves, closing the door behind him.

                     JOE
  How's freedom, kid, pretty fuckin' good, ain't it?
                     VIC
  It's a change.

                     JOE
  Ain't that a sad truth. Remy Martin?
                     VIC
  Sure.
                     JOE
  Take a seat.

Joe goes over to his liquor cabinet. Vic sits in a chair set in front of Joe's desk.

47

(while he pours the drinks)
Who's your parole officer?

VIC

A guy named Scagnetti. Seymour Scagnetti.

JOE

How is he?

VIC

, Fuckin' asshole, won't let me leave the halfway house.

Joe finishes pouring the drink; walks over and hands it to Vic.

JOE

Never ceases to amaze me. Fuckin' jungle bunny goes out there, slits some old woman's throat for twenty-five cents. Fuckin' nigger gets Doris Day as a parole officer. But a good fella like you gets stuck with a ball-bustin' prick.

Joe walks back around his desk and sits in his chair. Vic swallows some Remy.

VIC

I just want you to know, Joe, how much I appreciated your care packages on the inside.

JOE

What the hell did you expect me to do? Just forget about you?

VIC

I just wanted you to know, they meant a lot.

JOE

It's the least I could do, Vic. I wish I coulda done more.
(Joe flashes a wide grin at Vic)
Vic. Toothpick Vic. Tell me a story. What're your plans?

VIC

Well, what I wanna do is go back to work. But I got this Scagnetti   prick deep up my ass. He won't let me leave the halfway house till I get some piece of shit job. My plans have always been to be part of the team again.

There's a knock at the door.

JOE

Come in.

48

The door opens and in walks Joe's son, Nice Guy Eddie. Vic turns around in his seat and sees him.

EDDIE
(*to Vic*)
I see ya sittin' here, but I don't believe it.

Vic gets out of his seat and hugs Eddie.

How ya doin', Toothpick?

VIC
Fine, now.

EDDIE
I'm sorry man, I shoulda picked you up personally at the pen. This whole week's just been crazy. I've had my head up my ass the entire time.

VIC
Funny you should mention it. That's what your father and I been talkin' about.

EDDIE
That I should've picked you up?

49

No. That your head's been up your ass. I walk through the door
and Joe says, 'Vic, you're back, thank god. Finally somebody
who knows what the fuck he's doing. Vic, Vic, Vic, Eddie, my
son, is a fuck up.' And I say, 'Well, Joe, I coulda told you that.'
'I'm ruined! My son, I love him, but he's taking my business and
flushing it down the fuckin' toilet!'
(to Joe)
I'm not tellin' tales out of school. You tell 'im Joe. Tell 'im
yourself.

JOE

Eddie, I hate like hell for you to hear it this way. But when Vic
asked me how's business, well, you don't lie to a man who's just
done four years in the slammer for ya.

Eddie bobs his head up and down.

EDDIE

Oh really, is that a fact?

Eddie jumps Vic and they fall to the floor.

*The two friends, laughing and cussing at each other, wrestle on the floor
of Joe's office.*

Joe's on his feet yelling at them.

JOE
(yelling)

Okay, okay, enough, enough! Playtime's over! You wanna roll
around on the floor, do it in Eddie's office, not mine!

*The two men break it up. They are completely disheveled, hair a mess,
shirt-tails out. As they get themselves together, they continue to taunt one
another.*

EDDIE

Daddy, did ya see that?

JOE

What?

EDDIE

Guy got me on the ground, tried to fuck me.

VIC

You fuckin wish.

EDDIE

You tried to fuck me in my father's office, you sick bastard.
Look, Vic, whatever you wanna do in the privacy of your own
home, go to it. But don't try to fuck me. I don't think of you
that way. I mean, I like you a lot –

VIC

Eddie, if I was a pirate, I wouldn't throw you to the crew.

EDDIE

No, you'd keep me, for yourself. Four years fuckin' punks in the
ass made you appreciate prime rib when you get it.

VIC

I might break you, Nice Guy, but I'd make you my dog's bitch.
You'd be suckin' the dick and going down on a mangy T-bone
hound.

EDDIE

Now ain't that a sad sight, daddy, walks into jail a white man,
walks out talkin' like a nigger. It's all that black semen been
shootin' up his butt. It's backed up into his brain and comes out
of his mouth.

VIC

Eddie, you keep talkin' like a bitch, I'm gonna slap you like a
bitch.

JOE

Are you two finished? We were talkin' about some serious shit
when you came in, Eddie. We got a big problem we're tryin' to
solve. Now, Eddie, would you like to sit down and help us solve
it, or do you two wanna piss fart around?

*Playtime is over and Vic and Eddie know it. So they both take seats in
front of Joe's desk.*

Now Vic was tellin' me, he's got a parole problem.

EDDIE

Really? Who's your PO?

VIC

Seymour Scagnetti.

51

EDDIE

Scagnetti? Oh shit, I hear he's a motherfucker.

VIC

He is a fucker. He won't let me leave the halfway house till I get some piece of shit job.

EDDIE

You're coming back to work for us, right?

VIC

I wanna. But I gotta show this asshole I got an honest-to-goodness job before he'll let me move out on my own. I can't work for you guys and be worried about gettin' back before ten o'clock curfew.

JOE

(to Eddie)

We can work this out, can't we?

EDDIE

This isn't all that bad. We can give you a lot of legitimate jobs. Put you on the rotation at Long Beach as a dock worker.

VIC

I don't wanna lift crates.

EDDIE

You don't hafta lift shit. You don't really work there. But as far as the records are concerned, you do. I call up Matthews, the foreman, tell him he's got a new guy. Boom! You're on the schedule. You'll start getting a pay check at the end of the week. And ya know dock workers don't do too bad. So you can move into a halfway decent place without Scagnetti thinkin' 'What the fuck. Where's the money coming from?' And if Scagnetti ever wants to make a surprise visit, you're gone that day. That day we sent you to Tustin. 'Sorry, Scagnetti, we hadda bunch of shit out there we needed him to unload.' 'Tough luck, Seymour. You just missed him. We sent him to the Taft airstrip, five hours away, he's pickin' up a bunch of shit and bringing it back.' You see part of your job is goin' different places – and we got places all over the place.

JOE

(to Vic)

Didn't I tell ya not to worry?

52

                              (*To Eddie*)
Vic was worried.
                              EDDIE
Me and you'll drive down to Long Beach tomorrow. I'll introduce
you to Matthews, tell him what's going on.
                              VIC
That's great, guy, thanks a bunch.
                              (*pause*)
When do you think you'll need me for real work.
                              JOE
Well, it's kinda a strange time right now. Things are kinda –
                              EDDIE
– Nuts. We got a big meeting in Vegas coming up. And we're
kinda just gettin' ready for that right now.
                              JOE
Let Nice Guy set you up at Long Beach. Give ya some cash, get
that Scagnetti fuck off your back, and we'll be talking to ya.
                              EDDIE
Daddy, I got an idea. Now just hear it out. I know you don't like
to use any of the boys on these jobs, but technically Vic ain't one
of the boys. He's been gone for four years. He ain't on no one's
list. Ya know he can handle himself, ya know you can trust him.

Joe looks at Vic.

Vic has no idea what they're talking about.

                              JOE
How would you feel about pullin' a heist with about five other
guys?
FADE TO BLACK:

INT. NICE GUY EDDIE'S CAR (MOVING) – DAY

*Nice Guy Eddie is driving to the rendezvous talking on his portable car
phone. The sounds of the seventies are coming out of his car radio in the
form of 'Love Grows Where My Rosemary Goes' by Edison Lighthouse.*

                              EDDIE
                              (*into phone*)
Hey Dov, we got a major situation here.

                               53

(pause)

I know you know that. I gotta talk with Daddy and find out what
he wants done.

FLASH ON

INT. WAREHOUSE – DAY

*The Cop is standing in the warehouse with his hands cuffed behind his
back. Mr White, Mr Pink and Mr Blonde surround him and proceed to
beat the shit out of him. 'Love Grows . . .' Plays over the soundtrack.*

BACK TO NICE GUY EDDIE

EDDIE
(into phone)

All I know is what Vic told me. He said the place turned into a
fuckin' bullet festival. He took a cop as hostage, just to get the
fuck out of there.

FLASH ON

WAREHOUSE

The three men are stomping the cop into the ground.

BACK TO EDDIE

EDDIE
(into phone)

Do I sound like I'm jokin'? He's fuckin' driving around with the
cop in his trunk.

(pause)

I don't know who did what. I don't know who has the loot, if
anybody has the loot. Who's dead, who's alive, who's caught,
who's not . . . I will know, I'm practically there. But what do I tell
these guys about Daddy?

(pause)

Okay, that's what I'll tell em.

CUT TO:

54

EXT. WAREHOUSE – DAY

Three cars belonging to the other guys are parked outside the warehouse.

Eddie drives his car up to the warehouse. He gets out of the car, looks at the other cars parked outside.

> EDDIE
> (*to himself*)

Fucking assholes.

Eddie makes a beeline for the front door, bangs it open, and steps inside the warehouse.

INT. WAREHOUSE – DAY

The robbers have the cop tied to a chair and are still wailing on him.

Nice Guy Eddie walks in and everybody jumps.

> EDDIE

What in Sam Hill is goin' on?

Mr Pink and Mr White speak together.

> MR PINK

Hey, Nice Guy, we got a cop.

> WHITE
> (*at the same time*)

You're askin' what's goin' on? Where the fuck is Joe?

Nice Guy sees Mr Orange.

> EDDIE

Holy shit, Orange's all fucked up!

> WHITE

No shit, he's gonna fuckin' die on us if we don't get him taken care of.

> MR PINK

We were set up, the cops were waiting for us.

> EDDIE

What? Nobody set anybody up.

> MR PINK

The cops were there waitin' for us!

EDDIE

Bullshit.

MR PINK

Hey, fuck you, man, you weren't there, we were. And I'm tellin'
ya, the cops had that store staked out.

EDDIE

Okay, Mr Detective, who did it?

MR PINK

What the fuck d'you think we've been askin' each other?

EDDIE

And what are your answers? Was it me? You think I set you up?

MR PINK

I don't know, but somebody did.

EDDIE

Nobody did. You cowboys turn the jewelry store into a wild west
show, and you wonder why cops show up.

MR BLONDE

Where's Joseph?

EDDIE

I ain't talked to him. I talked to Dov. Dov said Daddy's comin'
down here, and he's fucking pissed.

MR PINK
(to Mr White)

I told ya he'd be pissed.

MR BLONDE

What did Joe say?

EDDIE

I told you, I haven't talked to him. All I know is, he's pissed.

MR WHITE
(pointing to Mr Orange)

What are you gonna do about him?

EDDIE

Jesus Christ, give me a fuckin' chance to breathe. I got a few
questions of my own, ya know.

MR WHITE

You ain't dying, he is.

EDDIE

I can see that, Mr Compassion. I'll call somebody.

57

MR WHITE

Who?

EDDIE

A snake charmer, what the fuck d'you think. I'll call a doctor, he'll fix 'm right up. No, where's Mr Brown and Mr Blue?

MR PINK

Brown's dead, we don't know about Blue.

EDDIE

Fuck, man. They killed Brown? Are you sure?

MR WHITE

Yeah I'm fuckin' sure, I was there. He took it in the face and in the neck.

EDDIE

And nobody's got a clue what happened to Mr Blue?

MR BLONDE

Well, he's either dead or he's alive or the cops got him or they don't.

Dolly to medium on the cop.

EDDIE

(off)

I take it this is the bastard you told me about.

(referring to the cop)

Why the hell are you beating the shit out of him?

MR PINK

So he'll tell us who the fuck set us up.

EDDIE

Would you stop it with that shit! You beat on this prick enough, he'll tell ya he started the Chicago fire. That don't necessarily make it so. Okay, first things fucking last, where's the shit? Please tell me somebody brought something with them.

MR PINK

I got a bag. I stashed it till I could be sure this place wasn't a police station.

EDDIE

Good for you. Well, let's go get it. We also gotta get rid of all those cars. It looks like Sam's hot car lot outside.

(pointing to Mr Blonde)

You stay here and babysit Orange and the cop.

(referring to Mr Pink and Mr White)
You two take a car each, I'll follow ya. You ditch it, I'll pick you
up, then we'll pick up the stones. And while I'm following you,
I'll arrange for some sort of a doctor for our friend.
MR WHITE
We can't leave these guys with him.
(meaning Mr Blonde)
EDDIE
Why not?

Mr White crosses to Mr Blonde.

MR WHITE
Because this guy's a fucking psycho. And if you think Joe's pissed
at us, that ain't nothing compared to how pissed off I am at him,
for puttin' me in the same room as this bastard.
MR BLONDE
(to Eddie)
You see what I been puttin' up with? As soon as I walk through
the door I'm hit with this shit. I tell 'em what you told me about us
stayin' put and Mr White whips out his gun, sticks it in my face,
and starts screaming, 'You motherfucker, I'm gonna blow you
away, blah, blah, blah.'
MR WHITE
He's the reason the place turned into a shooting gallery.
(to Mr Pink)
What are you, a silent partner? Fuckin' tell him.
MR PINK
He seems all right now, but he went crazy in the store.
MR WHITE
This is what he was doin'.

Mr White acts out Mr Blonde shooting everybody in the store.

MR BLONDE
I told 'em not to touch the alarm. They touched it. I blew 'em full
of holes. If they hadn't done what I told 'em not to, they'd still be
alive today.
MR WHITE
That's your excuse for going on a kill crazy rampage?

MR BLONDE

I don't like alarms.

EDDIE

What does it matter who stays with the cop? We ain't lettin' him go. Not after he's seen everybody. You should've never took him outta your trunk in the first place.

MR PINK

We were trying to find out what he knew about the set up.

EDDIE

There is no fuckin' set up!

(*Eddie takes charge*)

Look, this is the news. Blondie, you stay here and take care of them two. White and Pink come with me, 'cuz if Joe gets here and sees all those fucking cars parked out front, he's going to be as mad at me as he is at you.

Eddie, Mr White and Mr Pink walk out of the warehouse talking amongst themselves.

INT. WAREHOUSE – DAY – MR BLONDE AND COP

Mr Blonde closes the door after them. He then slowly turns his head towards the cop.

MR BLONDE

CU – COP'S FACE.

MR BLONDE
(*off*)

Now where were we?

COP

I told you I don't know anything about any fucking set up. I've only been on the force eight months, nobody tells me anything! I don't know anything! You can torture me if you want –

MR BLONDE
(*off*)

Thanks, don't mind if I do.

COP

Your boss even said there wasn't a set up.

60

MR BLONDE
(off)
First off, I don't have a boss. Are you clear about that?

He slaps the cop's face.

MR BLONDE
(off)
I asked you a question. Are you clear about that?
COP
Yes.

MR BLONDE
(off)
Now I'm not gonna bullshit you. I don't really care about what you know or don't know. I'm gonna torture you for a while regardless. Not to get information, but because torturing a cop amuses me. There's nothing you can say, I've heard it all before. There's nothing you can do. Except pray for a quick death, which you ain't gonna get.

He puts a piece of tape over the cop's mouth.

COP'S POV

Mr Blonde walks away from the cop.

MR BLONDE
Let's see what's on K-Billy's 'super sounds of the seventies' weekend.

He turns on the radio.

Stealer's Wheel's hit 'Stuck in the Middle with You' plays out the speaker.

Note: This entire sequence is timed to the music.

Mr Blonde slowly walks toward the cop. He opens a large knife.†

[He grabs a chair, places it in front of the cop and sits on it.]

Mr Blonde just stares into the cop's/our face, holding the knife, singing along with the song.

Then, like a cobra, he lashes out.

† Razor in completed film.
* Cut from completed film.

A slash across the face.

The cop/camera moves around wildly.

Mr Blonde just stares into the cop's/our face, singing along with the seventies hit.

Then he reaches out and cuts off the cop's/our ear.

The cop/camera moves around wildly.

Mr Blonde holds the ear up to the cop/us to see.

*[Mr Blonde rises, kicking the chair he was sitting on out of the way.]

INT./EXT. WAREHOUSE – DAY – HANDHELD SHOT

We follow Mr Blonde as he walks out of the warehouse . . . to his car. He opens the trunk, pulls out a large can of gasoline.

He walks back inside the warehouse . . .

INT. WAREHOUSE – DAY

. . . carrying the can of gas.

Mr Blonde pours the gasoline all over the cop, who's begging him not to do this.

Mr Blonde just sings along with Stealer's Wheel.

Mr Blonde lights up a match and, while mouthing:

> MR BLONDE
> 'Clowns to the left of me, jokers to the right. Here I am, stuck in the middle with you.'

He moves the match up to the cop . . .

. . . When a bullet explodes in Mr Blonde's chest.

The handheld camera whips to the right and we see the bloody Mr Orange firing his gun.

We cut back and forth between Mr Blonde taking bullet hits and Mr Orange emptying his weapon.

* Cut from completed film.

Mr Blonde falls down dead.

Mr Orange crawls to where the cop is, leaving a bloody trail behind him.

When he reaches the cop's feet he looks up at him.

> MR ORANGE
> (*feebly*)

What's your name?

> COP

Marvin.

> MR ORANGE

Marvin what?

> COP

Marvin Nash.

> MR ORANGE

Listen to me, Marvin Nash. I'm a cop.

> MARVIN

I know.

> MR ORANGE
> (*surprised*)

You do?

> MARVIN

Your name's Freddy something.

> MR ORANGE

Freddy Newendyke.

> MARVIN

Frankie Ferchetti introduced us once, about five months ago.

> MR ORANGE

Shit. I don't remember that at all.

> MARVIN

I do.

> (*pause*)

How do I look?

The gut-shot Mr Orange looks at the kid's gashed face and the hole in the side of his head where his ear use to be.

> MR ORANGE

I don't know what to tell you, Marvin.

Marvin starts to weep.

65

That fucking bastard! That fucking sick fucking bastard!

MR ORANGE

Marvin, I need you to hold on. There's officers positioned and
waiting to move in a block away.

MARVIN

(*screaming*)

What the fuck are they waiting for? That motherfucker cut off my
ear! He slashed my face! I'm deformed!

MR ORANGE

And I'm dying. They don't know that. All they know is they're
not to make a move until Joe Cabot shows up. I was sent
undercover to get Cabot. You heard 'em, they said he's on his
way. Don't pussy out on me now, Marvin. We're just gonna sit
here and bleed until Joe Cabot sticks his fuckin' head through that
door.

CUT TO:

TITLE CARD:

'MR ORANGE'

INT. DENNY'S – NIGHT

*A tough-looking black man named Holdaway, who sports a Malcolm X
beard, a green Chairman Mao cap with a red star on it, and a military
flack jacket, digs into a Denny bacon, cheese and avocado burger. He sits
in a booth all alone. He's waiting for somebody. As he waits, he
practically empties an entire bottle of ketchup on his french fries, not by
mistake either – that's just how he likes it.*

*We see Mr Orange, now known as Freddy Newendyke, wearing a high
school letterman jacket, enter the coffee shop, spot Holdaway, and head
his way. Holdaway sees Freddy bop towards him with a wide-ass
alligator grin plastered across his face.*

*Camera dollies fast down aisle to medium shot of Holdaway. We hear
Freddy off screen.*

FREDDY
(off)
Say 'hello' to a motherfucker who's inside. Cabot's doing a job and
take a big fat guess who he wants on the team?

HOLDAWAY
This better not be some Freddy joke.

LOW ANGLE
looking up at Freddy, who's standing at the table.

FREDDY
It ain't no joke, I'm in there. I'm up his ass.

CU – HOLDAWAY
Holdaway just looks at his pupil for a moment, then smiles.

HOLDAWAY
Congratulations.

EXT. DENNY – NIGHT

*Through the window of the restaurant we see Freddy slide into the booth
across from Holdaway. Freddy's doing a lot of talking, but we can't hear
what they're saying.*

INT. DENNY – NIGHT
FREEZE FRAME ON HOLDAWAY

*We are frozen on a medium close up of Holdaway listening to Freddy.
We hear restaurant noise and Freddy off screen.*

FREDDY
(off)
Nice Guy Eddie tells me Joe wants to meet me. He says I should
just hang around my apartment and wait for a phone call. Well,
after waiting three goddamn days by the fuckin' phone, he calls
me last night and says Joe's ready, and he'll pick me up in fifteen
minutes.

The freeze frame ends. Holdaway comes suddenly up to speed and says:

HOLDAWAY
Who all picked you up?

From here to end we cut back and forth.

FREDDY
Nice Guy. When we got to the bar . . .

HOLDAWAY
. . . What bar?

FREDDY
The Boots and Socks in Gardena. When we got there, I met Joe
and a guy named Mr White. It's a phony name. My name's Mr
Orange.

HOLDAWAY
You ever seen this motherfucker before?

FREDDY
Who, Mr White?

HOLDAWAY
Yeah.

FREDDY
No, he ain't familiar. He ain't one of Cabot's soldiers either. He's
gotta be from outta town. But Joe knows him real well.

HOLDAWAY
How can you tell?

FREDDY
The way they talk to each other. You can tell they're buddies.

HOLDAWAY
Did the two of you talk?

FREDDY
Me and Mr White?

HOLDAWAY
Yeah.

FREDDY
A little.

HOLDAWAY
What about?

FREDDY
The Brewers.

HOLDAWAY
The Milwaukee Brewers?

FREDDY
Yeah. They had just won the night before, and he made a killing
off 'em.

68

HOLDAWAY

Well, if this crook's a Brewers fan, his ass has gotta be from
Wisconsin. And I'll bet you everything from a diddle-eyed Joe to a
damned-if-I-know, that in Milwaukee they got a sheet on this Mr
White motherfucker's ass. I want you to go through the mugs of
guys from old Milwaukee with a history of armed robbery, and
put a name to that face.

Holdaway takes a big bite out of his burger.

(with his mouth full)

What kinda questions did Cabot ask?

FREDDY

Where I was from, who I knew, how I knew Nice Guy, had I done
time, shit like that.

*Holdaway's talked enough, he's eating his burger now. He motions for
Freddy to elaborate.*

He asked me if I ever done armed robbery before. I read him my
credits. I robbed a few gas and sips, sold some weed, told him
recently I held the shotgun while me and another guy pulled down
a poker game in Portland.

HOLDAWAY

How was Long Beach Mike's referal?

FREDDY

Perfecto! His backin' me up went a long fuckin' way. I told 'em it
was Long Beach Mike I did the poker game with. When Nice Guy
called him to check it out, he said I was A-okay. He told 'em I was
a good thief, I didn't rattle, and I was ready to make a move. What
happens to Long Beach Mike now?

HOLDAWAY

We'll take care of him.

FREDDY

Do right by him, he's a good guy. I wouldn't be inside if it wasn't
for him.

HOLDAWAY

Long Beach Mike isn't your amigo, he's a fuckin' scumbag. The
piece of shit is selling out his real amigos, that's how much of a
good fuckin' guy he is. We'll look after his ass, but get that no
good motherfucker outta mind, and tend to business.

Camera moves from a medium on Freddy to a closeup.

HOLDAWAY
(*off*)
Didja use the commode story?

FREDDY
Fuckin'-A. I tell it real good, too.

EXT. ROOFTOP — DAY

Freddy and Holdaway at one of their many rendezvous, an LA city rooftop.

FREDDY
What's this?

HOLDAWAY
It's a scene. Memorize it.

FREDDY
What?

HOLDAWAY
An undercover cop has got to be Marlon Brando. To do this job you got to be a great actor. You got to be naturalistic. You got to

70

be naturalistic as hell. If you ain't a great actor you're a bad actor, and bad acting is bullshit in this job.

FREDDY
(referring to the papers)
But what is this?

HOLDAWAY
It's an amusing anecdote about a drug deal.

FREDDY
What?

HOLDAWAY
Some funny shit that happened while you were doing a job.

FREDDY
I gotta memorize all this? There's over four fuckin' pages of shit here.

HOLDAWAY
It's like a fuckin' joke, man. You remember what's important and the rest you make your own. You can tell a joke, can't ya?

FREDDY
I can tell a joke.

HOLDAWAY
Well just think about it like that. Now the things you hafta remember are the details. It's the details that sell your story. Now your story takes place in a men's room. So you gotta know the details about that men's room. You gotta know if they got paper towels or a blower to dry your hands. You gotta know if the stalls got doors or not. You gotta know if they got liquid soap or that pink granulated powder shit. If they got hot water or not. If it stinks. If some nasty motherfucker sprayed diarrhea all over one of the bowls. You gotta know every damn thing there is to know about that commode. And the people in your story, you gotta know the details about them, too. Anybody can tell who did what to whom. But in real life, when people tell a story, they try to recreate the event in the other person's mind. Now what *you* gotta do is take all them details and make 'em your own. This story's gotta be about you, and how you perceived the events that took place. And the way you make it your own is you just gotta keep sayin' it and sayin' it and sayin' it and sayin' it and sayin' it.

INT. FREDDY'S APARTMENT – DAY

Freddy paces back and forth, in and out of frame, rehearsing the anecdote. He's reading it pretty good, but he's still reading it from the page, and every once in a while he stumbles over his words.

FREDDY

. . . this was during the Los Angeles marijuana drought of '86. I still had a connection. Which was insane, 'cause you couldn't get weed anyfuckinwhere then. Anyway, I had a connection with this hippie chick up in Santa Cruz. And all my friends knew it. And they'd give me a call and say, 'Hey, Freddy, you buyin' some, you think you could buy me some too?' They knew I smoked, so they'd ask me to buy a little for them when I was buyin'. But it got to be everytime I bought some weed, I was buyin' for four or five different people. Finally I said, 'Fuck this shit.' I'm makin' this bitch rich. She didn't have to do jack shit, she never even had to meet these people. I was fuckin' doin' all the work. So I got together with her and told her, 'Hey, I'm sick of this shit. I'm comin' through for everybody, and nobody's comin' through for me. So, either I'm gonna tell all my friends to find their own source, or you give me a bunch of weed, I'll sell it to them, give you the money, minus ten percent, and I get my pot for free.' So, I did it for a while . . .

Freddy exits frame.

CUT TO:

EXT. ROOFTOP – DAY

Another empty frame, except obviously outside. Freddy enters frame from the same direction he exited in the previous scene, finishing his sentence. When we move to a wider shot we see Freddy performing his monologue to Holdaway. Freddy paces back and forth as he performs his story.

FREDDY

. . . but then that got to be a pain in the ass. People called me on the phone all the fuckin' time. I couldn't rent a fuckin' tape without six phone calls interrupting me. 'Hey, Freddy when's the next time you're gettin' some?' 'Motherfucker, I'm tryin' to watch *Lost Boys* – when I have some, I'll let you know.' And then these

rinky-dink pot heads come by – they're my friends and
everything, but still. I got all my shit laid out in sixty dollar bags.
Well, they don't want sixty dollars worth. They want ten dollars
worth. Breaking it up is a major fuckin' pain in the ass. I don't
even know how much ten dollars worth is. 'Well, fuck, man, I
don't want that much around. If I have that much around I'll
smoke it.' 'Hey, if you guys can't control your smokin', that's not
my problem. You motherfuckers been smokin' for five years, be
adult about it.' Finally I just told my connection, count me out.
But as it turns out, I'm the best guy she had, and she depended
alot on my business. But I was still sick to death of it. And she's
tryin' to talk me into not quitin'.

Now this was a very weird situation, 'cause I don't know if you
remember back in '86 there was a major fuckin' drought. Nobody
had anything. People were livin' on resin and smokin' the wood in
their pipes for months. And this chick had a bunch, and was
beggin' me to sell it. So I told her I wasn't gonna be Joe the Pot
Man anymore. But I would take a little bit and sell it to my close,
close, close friends. She agreed to that, and said we'd keep the
same arrangement as before, ten percent and free pot for me, as
long as I helped her out that weekend. She had a brick of weed she
was sellin', and she didn't want to go to the buy alone.

CUT TO:

INT. BOOTS AND SOCKS BAR – NIGHT

*Freddy, Joe, Nice Guy Eddie and Mr White all sit around a table in a
red-lighted smokey bar. Freddy continues his story. The crooks are
enjoying the hell out of it.*

                    FREDDY
. . . Her brother usually goes with her, but he's in county
unexpectedly.
                    MR WHITE
What for?

                    FREDDY
Traffic tickets gone to warrant. They stopped him for something,
found the warrants on 'im, took 'im to jail. She doesn't want to
walk around alone with all that weed. Well, I don't wanna do this,

73

I have a bad feeling about it, but she keeps askin' me, keeps askin' me, finally I said okay 'cause I'm sick of listening to it. Well, we're picking this guy up at the train station.
                              JOE
You're picking the buyer up at the train station? You're carrying the weed on you?
                            FREDDY
Yeah, the guy needed it right away. Don't ask me why. So we get to the train station, and we're waitin' for the guy. Now I'm carrying the weed in one of those carry-on bags, and I gotta take a piss. So I tell the connection I'll be right back, I'm goin' to the little boys room . . .

CUT TO:

INT. MEN'S ROOM — TRAIN STATION — DAY

MEDIUM ON FREDDY
He walks through the door with a carry-on bag over his shoulder. Once he's inside, he stops in his tracks. We move into a closeup.

                            FREDDY
                          (*voice over*)
. . . So I walk into the men's room, and who's standing there?

FREEZE FRAME
on Freddy standing in front of four Los Angeles County Sheriffs and one German Shepherd. All of their eyes are on Freddy. Everyone is frozen.

                            FREDDY
                          (*voice over*)
. . . four Los Angeles County Sheriffs and a German Shepherd.
                      NICE GUY EDDIE
                          (*voice over*)
They were waitin' for you?
                            FREDDY
                          (*voice over*)
No. They were just a bunch of cops hangin' out in the men's room, talkin'. When I walked through the door they all stopped what they were talking about and looked at me.

74

BACK TO BAR

EXTREME CU – MR WHITE

                    MR WHITE
That's hard, man. That's a fuckin' hard situation.

BACK TO MEN'S ROOM

EXTREME CU GERMAN SHEPHERD

barking his head off.

                    FREDDY
                  (*voice over*)
The German Shepherd starts barkin'. He's barkin' at me. I mean
it's obvious he's barkin' at me.

*We do a slow 360 around Freddy in the men's room. We can hear the
dog barking.*

Every nerve ending, all of my senses, the blood in my veins,
everything I had was screaming, 'Take off, man, just take off,
get the fuck outta there!' Panic hit me like a bucket of water.
First there was the shock of it – BAM, right in the face! Then
I'm just stanin' there drenched in panic.

And all those sheriffs are lookin' at me and they know. They can
smell it. As sure as that fuckin' dog can, they can smell it on me.

FREEZE FRAME
*Freeze frame shot of Freddy standing in front of the sheriffs. It suddenly
jerks to life, and moves to speed. The dog is barking. Freddy moves to
his right, out of frame. We stay on the sheriffs. One sheriff yells at the
dog.*

                    SHERIFF #I
Shut up!

*The dog quietens down. Sheriff #2 continues with his story. A couple of
the sheriffs look over at Freddy off screen, but as Sheriff #2 talks, turn
their attention to him.*

So my gun's drawn, right? I got it aimed right at him. I tell 'im, 'Freeze, don't fuckin' move.' And the little idiot's lookin' at me, nodding his head 'Yes,' sayin', 'I know . . . I know . . . I know.' Meanwhile, his right hand is creepin' towards his glove box. So I scream at him, 'Asshole, you better fuckin' freeze right now!' And he's still lookin' at me, saying 'I know . . . I know . . . I know.' And his right hand's still going for the glove box.

The camera pans away from the sheriffs to Freddy, up against the urinal, playing possum, pretending to piss.

I tell 'im, 'Buddy, I'm gonna shoot you in the face right now if you don't put your hands on the fuckin' dash.' And the guy's girlfriend, a real sexy Oriental bitch, starts screamin' at him, 'Chuck, are you out of your mind? Put your hands on the dash like the officer said.' And then like nothing, the guy snaps out of it and casually puts his hands on the dash.

Freddy finishes his playing possum piss, and walks past the sheriffs over to the sink. The camera pans with him. A sheriff is sitting on a sink. He looks down and watches Freddy wash his hands.

SHERIFF #1
What was he goin' for?

SHERIFF #2
His registration. Stupid fuckin' citizen, doesn't have the slightest idea how close he came to gettin' shot.

Freddy finishes washing his hands. He goes to dry them, but there's only those hand drying machines. Freddy turns on the drying machine. He can't hear anything the sheriffs say now. The sound of the machine dominates the sound track.

These following shots are slow motion.

CU – FREDDY
CU – *his hands, rubbing each other getting blown dry.*

Shot of Sheriffs staring at Freddy.

CU – FREDDY

CU – FREDDY'S HANDS.

CU – GERMAN SHEPHERD

He barks. We can't hear him because of the machine. Machine turns off.
Freddy turns and walks out of the room.

BACK TO BAR

CU – JOE

> JOE
> (*laughing*)
> That's how you do it, kid. You knew how to handle that situation.
> You shit your pants, and then you just dive in and swim.

In slow motion Joe lights a cigar.

> HOLDAWAY
> (*off*)
> Tell me more about Cabot.

> FREDDY
> (*off*)
> He's a cool guy. A real nice, real funny, real cool guy.

CUT TO:

**[INT. DENNY'S – NIGHT

> FREDDY
> You remember *The Fantastic Four?*

> HOLLOWAY
> Yeah.

> FREDDY
> The Thing. The motherfucker looks just like The Thing.]

*[CUT TO:

INT. FREDDY'S APARTMENT – DAY

Freddy is sitting at a table, eating Captain Crunch, and flipping through
mug shots.

** Added during shooting.
* Cut from completed film.

78

CU – SOME UGLY MUGS

Then we come to Mr White's mug shot.

Freddy's recognition.

He grabs his phone, dials a number, and takes a quick spoonful of cereal before it's answered.

HOLDAWAY
(off)

Whatcha want?

FREDDY
(mouthful)

Jim?

HOLDAWAY
(off)

Who the fuck is this?

He swallows.

FREDDY

Freddy Newendyke.

HOLDAWAY
(off)

You find him yet, Newendyke?

79

FREDDY

I'm lookin' at him right now.

HOLDAWAY

(*off*)

So what's Mr White's real name?

FREDDY

Lawrence Dimick, D-I-M-I-C-K.

HOLDAWAY

(*off*)

Good work, Newendyke. We'll see what we can find out about Mr Dimick's ass.

CUT TO:

INT. COMPUTER ROOM – DAY

CU – COMPUTER SCREEN

the name Dimick, Lawrence is typed in.

CU – ENTER BUTTON IS PUNCHED

CU – FEMALE COMPUTER OPERATOR, JODIE McCLUSKEY

JODIE

This is your life, Lawrence Dimick!

CU – COMPUTER PRINTER

printing out sheet. The noise of the printer plays loud over the soundtrack. Jodie's hand comes into frame and tears sheet from the printer.

CUT TO:

EXT. HAMBURGER STAND – DAY

Freddy, Holdaway, and Jodie sit at a cabana table in front of a humburger stand, stuffing their faces with gigantic burgers.

HOLDAWAY

Read us what you got, McCluskey.

JODIE

Lawrence 'Larry' Dimick. Also known as Lawrence Jacobs and Alvin 'Al' Jacobs. This guy is Mr Joe-Armed-Robbery. He's a pro and he makes it a habit not to get caught. He's only been convicted twice, which is pretty good for somebody living a life of crime. Once for armed robbery, when he was twenty-one, in Milwaukee.

FREDDY

What was it?

JODIE

Payroll office at a lumber yard. First offense – he got eighteen months. He didn't get busted again until he was thirty-two. And then it was a backdoor bust. A routine vice squad roust. They roust this bar, our buddy Lawrence is in there knocking down a few. He gets picked up. He's wearing on his person an outlaw .45 automatic, apparently his weapon of choice. Also, on his finger is a diamond ring from a jewelry store robbery a year earlier. He got two years back inside for that.

Freddy winces.

FREDDY

Goddamn, that's hard time.

JODIE

So far, it's the only time he's ever done.

HOLDAWAY

Was this vice squad bullshit in Milwaukee?

JODIE

No. The vice squad roust was in LA. He's been in Los Angeles since '77.

FREDDY

When did he do this time?

JODIE

Back in '83, got out late '86. I found something else out I think you two should be aware of. About a year and a half ago, up in Sacramento, an undercover cop, John Dolenz, worked his way into a bank job. Apparently before the job they found out he was a cop. Now picture this: it's Dolenz's birthday, a bunch of cops are waiting in his apartment for a surprise party. The door opens, everyone yells 'Surprise!', and standing in the doorway is Dolenz and this other guy sticking a gun in Dolenz ribs. Before anybody knows what's going on, this stranger shoots Dolenz dead and starts firing two .45 automatics into the crowd.

HOLDAWAY

What happened?

JODIE

It was a mess. Cops got hit, wives got hit, girlfriends got hit, his dog got hit. People got glass in their faces. Three were killed, six were wounded.

FREDDY

They couldn't pin the killing on one of the bank robbers?

JODIE

They tried, but they didn't have a positive ID and all those guys had alibis. Besides, we really didn't have anything on them. We had the testimony of a dead man that they were talking about committing a robbery. They never went ahead with the bank job.

FREDDY

And Larry Dimick was one of the boys?

JODIE

He was probably the one.

HOLDAWAY

Just how sure are you with your cover?

FREDDY

Today they may know something, tomorrow they may know something else, but yesterday they didn't know anything. What's the next step.

HOLDAWAY

Do what they told ya. Sit in your apartment and wait for 'em to call you. We'll have guys posted outside who'll follow you when they pick you up.]

INT. FREDDY'S — DAY

CU — TELEPHONE
It rings. Freddy answers it, we follow the receiver up to his face.

FREDDY

Hello.

NICE GUY EDDIE
(*off — through phone*)

It's showtime. Grab your jacket —

82

INT. NICE GUY EDDIE'S CAR (PARKED) – DAY

CU – *Nice Guy Eddie speaking into the car phone*

                    EDDIE
– We're parked outside.

                    FREDDY
              (*off – through phone*)
I'll be right down.

Through the phone we hear the click of Freddy hanging up. Nice Guy places the receiver back in its cradle.

                    EDDIE
He'll be right down.

INT. FREDDY'S APARTMENT – DAY

The camera follows Freddy as he hops around the apartment getting everything he needs. He puts on his jacket and slips on some sneakers.

Before he goes he roots around among some coins on the table, finds his ring and puts it on.

Dolly fast toward the front door knob. Freddy's hand comes into frame, grabs the knob, then lets go. We move up to his face.

> FREDDY
> (*to himself*)
> Don't pussy out on me now. They don't know. They don't know shit.
> (*pause*)
> You're not gonna get hurt. You're fucking Baretta and they believe every word, cuz you're super cool.

He exits frame. We stay put and hear the door open and close off screen.

EXT. FREDDIE'S APARTMENT – DAY

COPS' POV

From inside an unmarked car across the street, the two cops watching Freddy see him walk out of his building and up to Eddie's parked car.

> COP #1
> (*off*)
> There goes our boy.

> COP #2
> (*off*)
> I swear, a guy has to have rocks in his head the size of Gibraltar to work undercover.

> COP #1
> (*off*)
> Do you want one of these?

> COP #2
> (*off*)
> Yeah, gimme the bear claw.

Freddy gets into the car and it pulls into traffic. Cop #1 starts the engine and follows.

INT. NICE GUY EDDIE'S CAR (MOVING) – DAY

Nice Guy Eddie is behind the wheel. Mr Pink is in the passenger seat. Freddy and Mr White are in the backseat together.

84

MR PINK

. . . Hey, I know what I'm talkin' about, black women ain't the same as white women.

MR WHITE
(*sarcastically*)
There's a slight difference.

The car laughs.

MR PINK

Go ahead and laugh, you know what I mean. What a white bitch will put up with, a black bitch won't put up with for a minute. They got a line, and if you cross it, they fuck you up.

EDDIE
I gotta go along with Mr Pink on this. I've seen it happen.

MR WHITE
Okay, Mr Expert. If this is such a truism, how come every nigger I know treats his woman like a piece of shit?

MR PINK
I'll make you a bet that those same damn niggers who were showin' their ass in public, when their bitches get 'em home, they chill the fuck out.

MR WHITE
Not these guys.

MR PINK
Yeah, those guys too.

EDDIE
Let me tell you guys a story. In one of Daddy's clubs there was this black cocktail waitress named Elois.

MR WHITE
Elois?

EDDIE
Yeah, Elois. E and Lois. We called her Lady E.

MR WHITE
Where was she from, Compton?

No. She was from Ladora Heights.

MR PINK

The black Beverly Hills. I knew this lady from Ladora Heights
once.
(*in a stuck up black female voice*)
'Hi, I'm from Ladora Heights, it's the black Beverly Hills.'

EDDIE

It's not the black Beverly Hills, it's the black Palos Verdes.
Anyway, this chick, Elois, was a man-eater-upper. I bet every guy
who's ever met her has jacked off to her at least once. You know
who she looked like? Christie Love. 'Member that TV show *Get
Christie Love*? She was a black female cop. She always used to say,
'You're under arrest, sugar.'

MR PINK

I was in the sixth grade when that show was on. I totally dug it.
What the fuck was the name of the chick who played Christie Love?

EDDIE

Pam Grier.

MR PINK

No, it wasn't Pam Grier, Pam Grier was the other one. Pam Grier
made the movies. *Christie Love* was like a Pam Grier TV show,
without Pam Grier.

MR PINK

What the fuck was that chick's name? Oh this is just great, I'm
totally fuckin' tortured now.

EDDIE

Well, whoever she was, Elois looked like her. So one night I walk
into the club, and no Elois. Now the bartender was a wetback, he
was a friend of mine, his name was Carlos. So I asked him, 'Hey,
Carlos, where's Lady E tonight?' Well apparently Lady E was
married to this real piece of dog shit. I mean, a real animal. And
apparently he would do things to her.

FREDDY

Do things? What would he do? You mean like beat her up?

EDDIE

Nobody knows for sure what he did. We just knew he did
something. Anyway, Elois plays it real cool. And waits for the next
time this bag of shit gets drunk. So one night the guy gets drunk and
passes out on the couch. So while the guy's inebriated, she strips
him naked. Then she takes some crazy glue and glues his dick to his
belly.

The car reacts to how horrible that would be.

I'm dead fuckin' serious. She put some on his dick and some on his
belly, then stuck 'em together. The paramedics had to come and cut
it loose.

The car reacts badly.

MR WHITE

Jesus Christ!

FREDDY

You can do some crazy things with it.

EDDIE

I don't know what he did to her, but she got even.

MR WHITE

Was he all pissed off?

MR PINK

How would you feel if you had to do a handstand every time you
took a piss.

The car laughs.

*[EXT. WAREHOUSE – DAY

*Nice Guy Eddie pulls up outside the warehouse. The four men climb out of
the car and follow Eddie inside.*

INT. WAREHOUSE – DAY

The four men enter the building.

* Cut from completed film.

87

At the other end of the warehouse, sitting in chairs, are Mr Blonde, Mr Brown, Mr Blue and Joe Cabot.

We shoot this from overhead, looking down on the men.

> JOE
> (*to everybody*)
> . . . So they're talkin about how they get their wives off, and the French guy says:
> (*in a bad French accent*)
> 'All I gotta do is take my pinky and tickle my Fifi's little oo-la-la and she rises a foot off the bed.'

Back to Joe.
> So the dago says:

CU – JOE

> (*in a good Brooklyn accent*)
> 'That's nothin'. When I take the tip of my tongue and wiggle it against my Mary Louise's little fun pimple, she rises two feet off da bed.' Then our friend from Poland says:
> (*in a dumb voice*)
> 'You guys ain't no cocksmen. When I get through fuckin' my Sophie, I wipe my dick on the curtains and you know what? She hits the roof!'

Joe laughs like a crazy man.

> Ha, ha, ha, ha, ha, ha!

We hear a lot of laughing off screen.

> Ain't that a masterpiece? Stupid fuckin' Polack, wipes his dick on the drapes.

Joe's eyes greet the new arrivals.

> You're here, great!

JOE EXITS – CU

We now have everybody from the Uncle Bob's Pancake House scene together again. The men sit on folding chairs, some stand. Joe sits in front of them on the edge of a table. A blackboard with a layout of the jewelry store is off to the right.

We do a 360 around the men.

EDDIE

We woulda gotten here sooner, but we got backed up around La
Brea and Pico.

JOE

No hurry.

(*to the boys*)

All right, let's get to know one another.]

**[INT. WAREHOUSE – DAY

JOE

You guys like to tell jokes and giggle and kid around, huh?
Giggling like a bunch of young broads in a school yard. Well, let
me tell a joke.

Camera tracks across the men's faces.

Five guys sitting in a bull pen, San Quentin. Wondering how the
fuck they got there. What'd we do wrong? What should we've
done? What didn't we do? It's your fault, my fault, his fault. All
that bullshit. Finally, someone comes up with the idea, wait a
minute, while we were planning this caper, all we did was sit
around and tell fucking jokes. Got the message? When this caper's
over, and I'm sure it's gonna be a successful one, hell, we'll go
down to the Hawaiian Islands and I'll roar and laugh with all of
you. You'll find me a different character down there. Right now
it's a matter of business.] With the exception of Eddie and myself,
who you already know, you'll be using aliases. Under no
circumstances are you to tell one another your real name or
anything else about yourself. That includes where you're from,
your wife's name, where you might've done time, about a bank in
St Petersburg you might've robbed. You guys don't say shit about
who you are, where you been or what you've done. Only thing you
guys can talk about is what you're going to do. This way the only
ones who know who the members of the team are are Eddie and
myself. And that's the way I like it. Because in the unlikely event
of one of you getting apprehended by the cops, not that I expect

** Added during shooting.

that to happen – it most definitely should not happen – it hasn't
happened, you don't have anything to deal with. You don't know
any names. You know my name, you know Eddie's name. That I
don't care about. You gotta prove it. I ain't worried. Besides, this
way you gotta trust me. I like that. I set this up and picked the men I
wanted for it. None of you came to me, I approached all of you. I
know you. I know your work, I know your reputation. I know you
as men. Except for this guy.

Joe points a finger at Freddy.

Freddy shits a brick.

But he's OK. If he wasn't OK, he wouldn't be here. Okay, let me
introduce everybody to everybody. But once again, at the risk of
being redundant, if I even think I hear somebody telling or
referring to somebody by their Christian name . . .
          (*Joe searches for the right words*)
. . . you won't want to be you. Okay, quickly.
          (*pointing at the men as he gives them a name*)
Mr Brown, Mr White, Mr Blonde, Mr Blue, Mr Orange, and Mr
Pink.

                          MR PINK
Why am I Mr Pink?

                          JOE
'Cause you're a faggot.
Everybody laughs.

                          MR PINK
Why can't we pick out our own color?

                          JOE
I tried that once, it don't work. You get four guys fighting over
who's gonna be Mr Black. Since nobody knows anybody else,
nobody wants to back down. So forget it, I pick. Be thankful you're
not Mr Yellow.

                          MR BROWN
Yeah, but Mr Brown? That's too close to Mr Shit.

Everybody laughs.

MR PINK

Yeah, Mr Pink sounds like Mr Pussy. Tell you what, let me be Mr Purple. That sounds good to me, I'm Mr Purple.

JOE

You're not Mr Purple, somebody from another job's Mr Purple. You're Mr Pink.

MR WHITE

Who cares what your name is? Who cares if you're Mr Pink, Mr Purple, Mr Pussy, Mr Piss . . .

MR PINK

Oh that's really easy for you to say, you're Mr White. You gotta cool-sounding name. So tell me, Mr White, if you think 'Mr Pink' is no big deal, you wanna trade?

JOE

Nobody's trading with anybody! Look, this ain't a goddamn fuckin' city council meeting! Listen up Mr Pink. We got two ways here, my way or the highway. And you can go down either of 'em. So what's it gonna be, Mr Pink?

MR PINK

Jesus Christ, Joe. Fuckin' forget it. This is beneath me. I'm Mr Pink, let's move on.

Camera leaves the team and goes to the blackboard with the layout of the jewelry store on it.

*[JOE

(*off*)

Okay, fellas, let's get into this.]

CUT TO:

**[JOE

I'll move on when I feel like it. All you guys got the goddamn message? I'm so goddamn mad I can hardly talk. Let's go to work.

Joe turns towards the blackboard.]

* Cut from completed film.
** Added during shooting.

92

*[EXT. BLEACHERS – DAY

Freddy and Holdaway sit on some bleachers in an empty little league baseball field.

HOLDAWAY

Okay, we're gonna station men across the street from Karina's Fine Jewelry. But their orders will be not to move in unless the robbery gets out of control. You gotta make sure they don't have to move in. You're inside to make sure that everything goes according to Hoyle. We have men set up a block away from the warehouse rendezvous. They got complete visibility of the exterior. So as soon as Joe Cabot shows up, we'll see it.

FREDDY

What's your visibility of the interior?

HOLDAWAY

We can't see shit on the inside. And we can't risk gettin' any closer for fear they'll spot us.

FREDDY

This is bullshit, Jim. I get all the fuckin' danger of having you guys in my back pocket but none of the safety.

HOLDAWAY

What's the matter, Newendyke? Job too tough for ya? No one lied to you. You always knew we'd hang back until Joe Cabot showed up.

FREDDY

Oh, this is great. You ain't giving me no fuckin' protection whatsoever. But you are giving me an attitude.

HOLDAWAY

Since when does an undercover cop have protection? Freddy, you came into this thing with your eyes wide open, so don't start screamin' blind man now. I understand you're nervous. I wish the warehouse had more visible windows, but it doesn't. We have to make do with the cards we're dealt.

FREDDY

I didn't say I wasn't gonna do it. I'm just remarking on how shitty the situation is!

* Cut from completed film.

93

HOLDAWAY

I don't mean to be harsh with ya, but I've found tough love works best in these situations. We have to get Joe Cabot in the company of the thieves and in the same vicinity as the loot. We don't care about these other bastards. We're willing to offer them good deals to testify against Cabot.

FREDDY

Isn't this risk unorthodox?

HOLDAWAY

What?

FREDDY

Letting them go ahead with the robbery?

HOLDAWAY

The whole idea behind this operation is to catch Joe Cabot red-handed. We bust these hired hands, we ain't accomplished shit. Letting them go through with the heist is a risk, but Cabot's jobs are very clean. We got people surrounding the perimeter. We got a guy and a gal on the inside posing as a couple shopping for rings. We could replace the employees with cops, but we'd run the risk of tipping 'em off.

FREDDY

That's out. They know the faces of who works what shift.

HOLDAWAY

These guys are professionals. We're professionals. It's a risk, but I think it's a calculated risk.]

EXT. KARINA'S FINE JEWELRY – DAY

We see shots without sound, of the outside of the jewelry store.

Customers coming and going. Store clerks waiting on customers through the windows.

While we look at this we hear, over the soundtrack, Mr White and Freddy talking off screen.

MR WHITE
(*voiceover*)
Let's go over it. Where are you?

FREDDY
(*voiceover*)
I stand outside and guard the door. I don't let anybody come in or go out.

MR WHITE
(*voiceover*)
Mr Brown.

FREDDY
(*voiceover*)
Mr Brown stays in the car. He's parked across the street till I give him the signal, then he pulls up in front of the store.

MR WHITE
(*voiceover*)
Mr Blonde and Mr Blue?

FREDDY
(*voiceover*)
Crowd control. They handle customers and employees in the display area.

INT. MR WHITE'S CAR (PARKED) – DAY

Mr White and Freddy sit in a car parked across the street from the jewelry store, staking it out.

MR WHITE
Myself and Mr Pink?

FREDDY
You two take the manager in the back and make him give you the diamonds. We're there for those stones, period. Since no display cases are being fucked with, no alarms should go off. We're out of there in two minutes, not one second longer. What if the manager won't give up the diamonds?

95

MR WHITE

When you're dealing with a store like this, they're insured up the
ass. They're not supposed to give you any resistance whatsoever. If
you get a customer or an employee who thinks he's Charles
Bronson, take the butt of your gun and smash their nose in. Drops
'em right to the floor. Everyone jumps, he falls down, screaming,
blood squirts out his nose. Freaks everybody out. Nobody says
fuckin' shit after that. You might get some bitch talk shit to ya. But
give her a look, like you're gonna smash her in the face next. Watch
her shut the fuck up. Now if it's a manager, that's a different story.
The managers know better than to fuck around. So if one's givin'
you static, he probably thinks he's a real cowboy. So what you gotta
do is break that son-of-a-bitch in two. If you wanna know
something and he won't tell you, cut off one of his fingers. The little
one. Then you tell 'im his thumb's next. After that he'll tell ya if he
wears ladies underwear. I'm hungry, let's get a taco.

CUT TO:

EXT. ALLEY – DAY

It's the moment of the robbery. The alley is empty.

*In the distance we hear all hell breaking loose. Guns firing, people shouting
and screaming, sirens wailing, glass breaking . . .*

A car whips around the corner, into the alley.
The doors burst open, Freddy and Mr White hop out.

*Freddy opens the driver's side door. A bloody screaming Mr Brown falls
out.*

MR BROWN
(*screaming*)
My eyes! My eyes! I'm blind, I'm fucking blind!

FREDDY
You're not blind, there's just blood in your eyes.

*Mr White loads his two .45 automatics. He runs to the end of the alley just
as a police car comes into sight.*

Firing both .45s, Mr White massacres everyone in the patrol car.

96

Freddy, holding the dying Mr Brown, looks on at Mr White's ambush in shock.

Mr Brown lifts his head up, blood in his eyes.

MR BROWN

Mr Orange? You're Mr Orange, aren't you?

By the time Freddy turns his head back to him, Mr Brown is dead.

Mr White runs up to Freddy.

MR WHITE

Is he dead?

Freddy doesn't answer, he can't.

MR WHITE

Did he die or not?

Freddy, scared.

FREDDY

I'm sorry.

MR WHITE

What? Snap out of it!

Mr White grabs Freddy by the coat and yanks him along as he runs.

They exit the alley and flee down a street.

A car with a female driver comes up on the two men.

Mr White jumps in her path, stopping the car. He points his gun at her.

MR WHITE

Hold it! Hold it! Right there.

Freddy comes towards the driver's side of the car.

The Female Driver comes up with a gun from the glove compartment.

MR WHITE

Get out of the fucking car!

She shoots Freddy in the stomach.

On instinct Freddy brings up his gun and shoots her in the face.

CU – FREDDY
as he falls to the ground he realizes what's happened to him and what he's done.

Mr White drags the dead Female Driver out of the car. He shoves Freddy in the backseat and drives away.

INT. GETAWAY CAR (MOVING) – DAY

Freddy, holding his stomach and doubled over in pain, is crying.

We replay the scene between Freddy and Mr White in the getaway car. Except this time, we never leave Freddy.

>   MR WHITE
>   (*off*)
> Just hold on, buddy boy.

>   FREDDY
> I'm sorry. I can't believe she killed me . . .

CUT FROM FREDDY IN THE BACKSEAT TO:

*[INT. NICE GUY EDDIE'S CAR (MOVING) – DAY

Mr Pink is behind the wheel, Nice Guy Eddie is in the passenger seat going through the satchel with the diamonds. Mr White is in the backseat. The car is speeding back to the garage.

>   EDDIE
>   (*looking through the case*)
> You know, all things considered, this was pretty successful.

>   MR WHITE
> I don't believe you just said that.

>   EDDIE
> No, it was messy as hell, but do you realize how much you got away with? There's over two million dollars worth of diamonds here.

>   MR PINK
> I love this guy.

* Cut from completed film

99

EDDIE

Hey, what's done is done. We can all sit around and have a big cry
about it or we can deal with the situation at hand.

MR WHITE

The situation at hand isn't that fuckin' satchel. You and Joe have a
responsibility to your men.

EDDIE

Hey, it's the best I could do.

MR WHITE

The man is fucking dying.

EDDIE

And I'm telling you, Bonnie'll take care of him.

MR WHITE

He needs a doctor, not a fuckin' nurse.

EDDIE

Ask me how many doctors I called. You wanna embarrass yourself,
ask me how many doctors I called.

MR WHITE

Obviously not enough.

EDDIE

Fuck you! You gotta little black book, then whip it out. If not,
listen how it is. I called three doctors and couldn't get through to
shit. Now, time being a factor, I called Bonnie. Sweet broad,
helluva broad, and a registered nurse. Told her a bullshit story,
upside; she said bring him to her apartment.

MR WHITE

If he dies I'm holding you personally responsible.

EDDIE

Fuck you, buddy boy! Okay, you wanna play that way. I am
personally leaving myself vulnerable with this Bonnie situation. I
don't think she'll call the cops, but I don't know for sure. But me
being too nice-a-fuckin-guy was willin' to risk it. But no fuckin'
more.

(*he grabs his portable phone*)

I'm callin' Bonnie back and tellin' her to forget it. You take care of
your friend, you know so much about it.

MR PINK

Goddammnit, will you guys grow up!

EDDIE

I don't need to grow up, my friend. I am a grown up. I'm being
responsible, I'm taking care of business.

MR WHITE

Cut the shit! I don't think you called anybody except some cooze
you once fucked, who happens to wear orthopaedic shoes. And I
don't think that's good enough care for a gut-shot man.

EDDIE

Yeah, well I don't give a flying fuck what you think!

MR PINK
(to Mr White)

Look, he's not sayin' this bitch is gonna operate on him. She's
gonna give him better attention than we can until we can get a
doctor. Nobody's forgotten about doctors. Joe'll get one in a snap.
This is something we're doing in the meantime. I think both of you
are actin' like a couple of assholes.

EDDIE

Yeah, right. I arrange a nurse, I leave myself wide open, and I'm an
asshole.]

INT. WAREHOUSE – DAY

*Medium shot on the door. Nice Guy Eddie, Mr White and Mr Pink walk
through it. They stop in their tracks.*

*We see what they see. Mr Blonde, lying on the ground, shot full of holes.
The cop slumped over in his chair, a bloody mess, Mr Orange lying at the
cop's feet, holding his wound. Eddie, Mr White and Mr Pink walk into the
shot.*

EDDIE

What the fuck happened here?

Eddie runs over to his friend Mr Blonde/Toothpick Vic.

MR WHITE
(*to Mr Orange*)
What happened?

MR ORANGE
(*very weakly*)
Blonde went crazy. He slashed the cop's face, cut off his ear and
was gonna burn him alive.

EDDIE
(*yelling*)
Who cares what he was gonna do to this fuckin' pig?

*Eddie whips out his gun and shoots the cop. The cop and the chair tip
over. Eddie stands over him and shoots him once more.*

EDDIE
(to Mr Orange)
You were saying he went crazy? Something like that? Worse or
better?

MR ORANGE
Look, Eddie, he was pullin' a burn. He was gonna kill the cop and
me. And when you guys walked through the door, he was gonna
blow you to hell and make off with the diamonds.

MR WHITE
(*to Eddie*)
Uhuh, uhuh, what'd I tell ya? That sick piece of shit was a stone
cold psycho.

MR ORANGE
(*to Eddie*)
You could've asked the cop, if you didn't just kill him. He talked
about what he was going to do when he was slicing him up.

EDDIE
I don't buy it. It doesn't make sense.

MR WHITE
It makes perfect fuckin' sense to me. Eddie, you didn't see how he
acted during the job, we did.

Mr Pink walks over to the cop's body.

MR PINK
He's right about the ear, it's hacked off.

EDDIE
(to Mr Orange)
Let me say this out loud, just to get it straight in my mind.
According to you, Mr Blonde was gonna kill you. Then when we
came back, kill us, grab the diamonds, and scram. That's your
story? I'm correct about that, right?

MR ORANGE
Eddie, you can believe me or not believe me, but it's the truth. I
swear on my mother's eternal soul that's what happened.

The camera moves into a closeup of Nice Guy Eddie.

There's a long pause while he rolls over what Mr Orange has said. Finally:

*[EDDIE
You're a fuckin' liar. Now why don't you drop the fuckin' fairy tale
and tell me what really happened?

MR WHITE
(off)
He told you what really happened. You just can't deal with it.

MR ORANGE
(off)
Okay, you're right, I'm lying. Even though I'm fuckin' dyin' I'm
not above pullin' a fast one. Get rid of Blonde, we share his split –
no, scratch that, I shot him 'cause I didn't like his hair style. I didn't
like his shoes either. If it had just been his hair, I'd've maybe, maybe I
said, let him live. But hair and footwear together, he's a goner.]

EDDIE
The man you killed was just released from prison. He got caught at
a company warehouse full of hot items. He could've walked away.
All he had to do was say my dad's name. But instead he shut his
mouth and did his time. He did four years for us, and he did 'em
like a man. And we were very grateful. So, Mr Orange, you're
tellin' me this very good friend of mine, who did four years for my
father, who in four years never made a deal, no matter what they

* Cut from completed film.

103

dangled in front of him, you're telling me that now, that now this man is free, and we're making good on our commitment to him, he's just gonna decide, right out of the fuckin' blue, to rip us off?

Silence.

Mr Orange, why don't you tell me what really happened?

                          VOICE
Why? It'll just be more bullshit.

Eddie steps out of his closeup and we see Joe Cabot standing in the warehouse doorway. He walks into the room.

                          JOE
                  (*pointing to Mr Orange*)
    This man set us up.

Camera does a 360 around the men.

                          EDDIE
Daddy, I'm sorry, I don't know what's happening.

                          JOE
That's okay, Eddie, I do.

                       MR WHITE
What the fuck are you talking about?

                          JOE
                  (*pointing at Mr Orange*)
That piece of shit. Workin' with the cops.

              MR WHITE, MR PINK, EDDIE
What?

                          JOE
I said this lump of shit is workin' with the LAPD.

MR ORANGE'S POV

Looking up from the floor at everybody.

Joe looks down at Mr Orange.

                          JOE
    Aren't you?

MR ORANGE
(*off*)
I don't have the slightest fuckin' idea what you're talkin about.

MR WHITE
(*very calmly to Joe*)
Joe, I don't know what you think you know, but you're wrong.

JOE
Like hell I am.

MR WHITE
(*very calmly*)
Joe, trust me on this, you've made a mistake. He's a good kid. I
understand you're hot, you're super-fuckin' pissed. We're all real
emotional. But you're barking up the wrong tree. I know this man,
and he wouldn't do that.

JOE
You don't know jack shit. I do. This rotten bastard tipped off the
cops and got Mr Brown and Mr Blue killed.

MR PINK
Mr Blue's dead?

JOE

Dead as Dillinger.

EDDIE

The motherfucker killed Vic.

MR WHITE

How do you know all this?

JOE

He was the only one I wasn't a hundred per cent on. I should have
my fucking head examined for goin' forward when I wasn't a
hundred per cent. But he seemed like a good kid, and I was
impatient and greedy and all the things that fuck you up.

MR WHITE
(screaming)

That's your proof?

JOE

You don't need proof when you got instinct. I ignored it before, but
not no more.

He whips out a revolver and aims it at Mr Orange.

Mr White brings his .45 up at Joe.
Eddie and Mr Pink are shook awake by the flash of firearms.

Eddie raises his gun, pointing it at Mr White.

EDDIE

Have you lost your fucking mind? Put your gun down!

Mr Pink fades into the background, wanting no part of this.

MR WHITE

Joe, you're making a terrible mistake I can't let you make.

EDDIE

Stop pointing your fuckin' gun at Daddy!

We get many different angles of the Mexican standoff.

MEDIUMS ON EVERYBODY

Mr Orange holding his belly, looking from left to right.

Joe pointing down on Mr Orange. Not taking his eyes off him.

Mr White pointing at Joe, looking like he's ready to start firing any minute.

Eddie scared shitless for his father, gun locked on Mr White.

Mr Pink walking backwards, away from the action.

Nobody says anything.

FOUR SHOT
of guys ready for violence. Mr Pink in the background.

> MR PINK
>
> C'mon, guys, nobody wants this. We're supposed to be fuckin' professionals!

Joe raises his head to Mr White.

> JOE
>
> Larry, I'm gonna kill him.

> MR WHITE
>
> Joe, if you kill that man, you die next. Repeat, if you kill that man, you die next!

> EDDIE
>
> Larry, we have been friends and you respect my dad and I respect you, but I will put fucking bullets right through your heart. You put that fucking gun down.

> MR WHITE
>
> Goddamn you, Joe, don't make me do this.

> EDDIE
>
> Larry, stop pointing that fucking gun at my dad!

Joe fires three times, hitting Mr Orange with every one.

Mr White shoots Joe twice in the face. Joe brings his hands up to his face, screaming, and falls to the ground.

Eddie fires at Mr White, hitting him three times in the chest.

Mr White brings his gun around to Eddie and shoots him.

The two men fall to their knees, firing at each other.

Eddie collapses, dead.

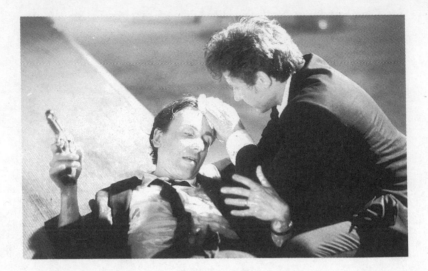

Joe's dead.

Mr Orange lies perfectly still, except for his chest heaving. The only sound we hear is his loud breathing.

Mr White is shot full of holes, but still on his knees, not moving.

Mr Pink is standing motionless. Finally he grabs the satchel of diamonds and runs out the door.

*[We hear outside a car start. Then the sound of a bullhorn yells out:

POLICE FORCE
(off)

Freeze! Get out of the car and lie face down on the ground!

MR PINK
(off)

Don't shoot!]

We now hear sirens, the sounds of more cars driving up, men running to the warehouse.

While all this noise is going on, Mr White tries to stand but falls down. He somehow makes it to where Mr Orange lies.

* Cut from completed film.

He lifts Mr Orange's head, cradling it in his lap and stroking his brow.

MR WHITE
(*with much effort*)
Sorry, kid. Looks like we're gonna do a little time.

Mr Orange looks up at him and, with even more of an effort:

MR ORANGE
I'm a cop.

Mr White doesn't say anything, he keeps stroking Orange's brow.

I'm sorry, I'm so sorry.

Mr White lifts his .45 and places the barrel between Mr Orange's eyes. The camera moves into an extreme closeup of Mr White.

The sounds of outside storm inside. We don't see anything, but we hear a bunch of shotguns cocking.

POLICE FORCE
(*off*)
Freeze, motherfucker! Drop your fucking gun! Drop the gun! Don't do it!

Mr White looks up at them, smiles, pulls the trigger.

BANG

We hear a burst of shotgun fire.

Mr White is blown out of frame, leaving it empty.

True Romance

'His films are a desperate cry from the heart of a grotesque fast-food culture.'
                                    – French critics on the films of Roger Corman

'. . . Beyond all the naïveté and stupidity, beyond the vulgarity inherent in the amount of money involved, beyond all this, a certain grandeur had rooted itself into the scheme, and I could still spy a reckless and artistic splendour to the way we had carried it out.'
                                    – Clifford Irving on the Howard Hughes hoax

Clarence (Christian Slater)

Alabama (Patricia Arquette)

INTRODUCTION

Quentin Tarantino on:

BEGINNINGS

The first script I ever did was *True Romance*. I wrote it to do the way
the Coen brothers did *Blood Simple*, and I almost directed it. Me
and a friend, Roger Avary, were going to raise about $1.2 million,
form a limited partnership and then go off and make the movie. We
worked on it for three years, trying to get it off the ground like that,
and it never worked. I then wrote *Natural Born Killers*, again hoping
to direct it myself, this time for half a million dollars – I was shooting
lower and lower. After a year and a half I was no further along than
at the beginning. It was then, out of frustration, that I wrote
Reservoir Dogs. I was going to go really guerrilla-style with it, like the
way Nick Gomez did *Laws of Gravity*. I'd lost faith in anyone giving
me money – and then that's *when* I got the money.

After *Reservoir Dogs* I was offered both of them to direct. The
producers who had *Natural Born Killers* – before Oliver Stone
acquired it – tried like hell to talk me into directing it. Tony Scott
and Bill Unger had *True Romance*. I had convinced Tony to direct it,
but Bill was saying, 'Look, Quentin, would you be interested in
doing this as a follow-up to *Reservoir Dogs*?' And my answer was no.
I didn't want to do either one of them because they were both
written to be my first film and by then I'd made my first film. I
didn't want to go backwards and do old stuff. I think of them as old
girlfriends: I loved them, but I didn't want to marry them any more.
The thing that I am happiest about is that the first film of mine
produced was one that I directed.

STRUCTURE

True Romance had a complicated structure to start with, but when
the producers bought the script, they cut-and-pasted it into a linear
form. The original structure was also an answers-first, questions-
later structure, like *Reservoir Dogs*. Tony Scott actually started
putting it together that way in the editing room, but he said it didn't
work for him. I guess what I'm always trying to do is use these
structures that I see in novels and apply them to cinema. A novelist
thinks nothing of starting in the middle of a story. I thought that if

you could figure out a cinematic way to do that, it would be very exciting. Generally, when they translate novels to movies, that's the first stuff that goes out. I don't do this to be a wise guy or to show how clever I am. If a story would be more dramatically engaging if it were told from the beginning, or the end, then I'd tell it that way. But the *glory* is in pulling it off my way.

OMISSION

What you leave out is as crucial as what you put in. To me, omission even applies to the way you frame a shot. What you don't see in the frame is as important as what you do see. Some people like to show everything. They don't want the audience to have a second guess about anything; it's *all* there. I'm not like that. I've seen so many movies that I like playing around with them. Pretty much nine out of ten movies you see let you know in the first ten minutes what kind of movie it's going to be, and I think the audience subconsciously reads this early ten-minute message and starts leaning to the left when the movie is getting ready to make a left turn; they're predicting what the movie is going to do. And what I like to do is use that information against them. *Natural Born Killers* opens with a lazy coffee-shop scene that suddenly turns into a massacre. In *True Romance*, Alabama has a terrifying fight with a hit man. One of the reasons that I think that that scene is so exciting is because dramatically, in the context of where it falls in the movie, Alabama could get killed. We like Alabama, but it's getting towards the end of the movie and it would make a lot of sense for her to die. It would give Clarence something to do for the last fifteen minutes – avenge her.

I once saw this Stephen King movie called *Silver Bullet*, with Gary Busey. It's got this little kid in a wheelchair and this young girl who's narrating the story. At the end, there's a big fight with a werewolf – and I was so scared for Gary Busey! I knew they weren't going to kill the little kid in the wheelchair or the girl because she's the narrator, but Gary Busey *could* die. Dramatically, they could have killed him – and so it was really scary. My sympathy was with him, because he was perishable. The point is, I didn't know what was going to happen.

HEROES *and* VILLAINS

Throughout *True Romance*, Clarence and Alabama keep running into all these people, and when they do, the movie becomes the story of the people they meet. When they're with Clarence's father, I treat him as though the whole movie is going to be about him. When Vicenzo Coccotti, the gangster that Christopher Walken plays, comes in, the whole movie could be about him. The same thing with Drexl, the Gary Oldman character. But particularly the father – you just figure he's going to play a central role. One of the things I don't like about comedy-action films is comic villains. They're never a threat; they're usually just buffoonish. The villains in *True Romance* rub Dennis Hopper out. That's a shock. All right – so now these guys are really, really scary, and every time they come in you think the worst thing in the world could happen.

VIOLENCE

I don't take the violence very seriously. I find violence very funny, especially in the stories that I've been telling recently. Violence is part of this world and I am drawn to the outrageousness of real-life violence. It isn't about people lowering people from helicopters on to speeding trains, or about terrorists hijacking something or other. Real-life violence is, you're in a restaurant and a man and his wife are having an argument and all of a sudden that guy gets so mad at her, he picks up a fork and stabs her in the face. That's really crazy and comic bookish – but it also *happens*; that's how real violence comes kicking and screaming into your perspective in real life. I am interested in the act, in the explosion, and in the entire aftermath of that. What do we do after this? Do we beat up the guy who stabbed the woman? Do we separate them? Do we call the cops? Do we ask for our money back because our meal has been ruined? I am interested in answering all those questions.

To me, violence is a totally aesthetic subject. Saying you don't like violence in movies is like saying you don't like dance sequences in movies. I do like dance sequences in movies, but if I didn't, it doesn't mean I should stop dance sequences being made. When you're doing violence in movies, there's going to be a lot of people who aren't going to like it, because it's a mountain they can't climb. And they're not *jerks*. They're just not into that. And they don't *have* to be into it. There's other things that they can see. If you *can* climb that mountain, then I'm going to give you something to climb.

118

MORALITY

I'm not trying to preach any kind of morals or get any kind of message across, but for all the wildness that happens in my movies, I think that they usually lead to a moral conclusion. For example, I find what passes between Mr White and Mr Orange at the end of *Reservoir Dogs* very moving and profound in its morality and its human interaction.

ENDINGS

In my original script, Clarence gets killed. If I were to write a script and sell it now, I would make the provision that they wouldn't change anything. I can do that now, but at the time I was selling *True Romance* to get the money to make *Reservoir Dogs* it never occurred to me it would get changed. When I read the new ending, in which Clarence survives, I felt that it worked – I just didn't think it was as good an ending as mine. My ending has a symmetry with the whole piece. At first, I was really distraught about it; in fact, I was talking about taking my name off the film. I had a lot of faith in Tony Scott – I'm a big fan of his work, especially *Revenge* – but where I was coming from, you just couldn't change my ending.

Anyway, we got together and talked about it, and Tony said that he wanted to change the ending in particular, not for commercial reasons, but because he really liked these kids and he wanted to see them get away. He said, 'Quentin, I'm going to defer to you. I'm going to shoot both endings, then I'm going to look at them, and then decide which one I want to go with.' As much as I didn't want my ending changed, I figured I couldn't really ask for more than that. When it came to it, he really liked the happy ending and went with it.

CODA

True Romance is probably my most personal script because the character of Clarence was me at the time I wrote it. He works at a comic book shop – I was working in a video store. When my friends from that time see *True Romance*, they get melancholy; it brings back a certain time for us. It was weird when I first saw the movie because it was like looking at a big-budget version of my home movies, or memories.

119

True Romance was released in 1993.

The cast included:

CLARENCE WORLEY	Christian Slater
ALABAMA WHITMAN	Patricia Arquette
CLIFFORD WORLEY	Dennis Hopper
MENTOR (ELVIS)	Val Kilmer
DREXL SPIVEY	Gary Oldman
FLOYD	Brad Pitt
VINCENZO COCCOTTI	Christopher Walken
ELLIOT BLITZER	Bronson Pinchot
BIG DON	Samuel L. Jackson
DICK RITCHIE	Michael Rapaport
NICKY DIMES	Chris Penn
CODY NICHOLSON	Tom Sizemore
Written by	Quentin Tarantino
Directed by	Tony Scott
Produced by	Bill Unger
	Steve Perry
	Samuel Hadida
Director of Photography	Jeffrey L. Kimball
Art Director	James J. Murakami
Costume Design	Susan Becker
Editors	Michael Tronick
	Christian Wagner
Music	Hans Zimmer

A Morgan Creek production
Released through Warner Bros.

INT. BAR – NIGHT

A smoky cocktail bar in downtown Detroit.

Clarence Worley, a young hipster hepcat, is trying to pick up on an older lady named Lucy. She isn't bothered by him, in fact, she's a little charmed. But, you can tell that she isn't going to leave her barstool.

CLARENCE

In 'Jailhouse Rock' he's everything rockabilly's about. I mean, he is rockabilly: mean, surly, nasty, rude. In that movie he couldn't give a fuck about anything except rockin' and rollin', livin' fast, dyin' young, and leaving a good-lookin' corpse. I love that scene where after he's made it big he's throwing a big cocktail party, and all these highbrows are there, and he's singing, 'Baby You're So Square . . . Baby, I Don't Care.' Now, they got him dressed like a dick. He's wearing these stupid-lookin' pants, this horrible sweater. Elvis ain't no sweater boy. I even think they got him wearin' penny loafers. Despite all that shit, all the highbrows at the party, big house, the stupid clothes, he's still a rude-lookin' motherfucker. I'd watch that hillbilly and I'd want to be him so bad. Elvis looked good. I'm no fag, but Elvis was good-lookin'. He was fuckin' prettier than most women. I always said if I ever had to fuck a guy . . . I mean *had* too 'cause my life depended on it . . . I'd fuck Elvis.

Lucy takes a drag from her cigarette.

LUCY

I'd fuck Elvis.

CLARENCE

Really?

LUCY

When he was alive. I wouldn't fuck him now.

CLARENCE

I don't blame you.

121

(*they laugh*)
So we'd both fuck Elvis. It's nice to meet people with common interests, isn't it?

Lucy laughs.

Well, enough about the King, how 'bout you?

LUCY

How 'bout me what?

CLARENCE

How 'bout you go to the movies with me tonight?

LUCY

What are we gonna go see?

CLARENCE

A Sonny Chiba triple feature. *The Streetfighter, Return of the Streetfighter,* and *Sister Streetfighter.*

LUCY

Who's Sonny Chiba?

CLARENCE

He is, bar none, the greatest actor working in martial arts movies ever.

LUCY
(*not believing this*)
You wanna take me to a kung fu movie?

CLARENCE
(*holding up three fingers*)
Three kung fu movies.

Lucy takes a drag from her cigarette.

LUCY
(*laughing*)
I don't think so. Not my cup of tea.

TITLE SEQUENCE

TITLE CARD:

'MOTORCITY'

INT. DINGY HOTEL ROOM – DAY

The sounds of the city flow in through an open window: car horns, gun shots and voices. Paint is peeling off the walls and the once green carpet is stained black.

On the bed nearby is a huge open suitcase filled with clear plastic bags of cocaine. Shotguns and pistols have been dropped carelessly around the suitcase. On the far end of the room, against the wall, is a TV. Bewitched is playing.

At the opposite end of the room, by the front door, is a table. Drexl Spivey and Floyd Dixon sit around it. Cocaine is on the table as well as little plastic bags and a weigher. Floyd is black, Drexl is a white boy, though you wouldn't know it to listen to him.

DREXL
Nigger, get outta my face with that bullshit.

FLOYD
Naw man, I don't be eatin' that shit.

DREXL
That's bullshit.

Big Don Watts, a stout, mean-looking black man who's older than Drexl and Floyd, walks through the door carrying hamburgers and french fries in two greasy brown-paper bags.

FLOYD
Naw man that's some serious shit.

DREXL
Nigger, you lie like a big dog.

BIG D
What the fuck are you talkin' about?

DREXL
Floyd say he don't be eatin' pussy.

BIG D
Shit, any nigger say he don't eat pussy is lyin' his ass off.

DREXL

I heard that.

FLOYD

Hold on a second, Big D. You sayin' you eat pussy?

BIG D

Nigger, I eat everything. I eat the pussy. I eat the butt. I eat every motherfuckin' thang.

DREXL

Preach on, Big D.

FLOYD

Looky here. If I ever did eat some pussy – I would never eat any pussy – but, if I did eat some pussy, I sure as hell wouldn't tell no goddamn body. I'd be ashamed as a motherfucker.

BIG D

Shit! Nigger, you smoke enough sherm your dumb ass'll do a lot a crazy ass things. So you won't eat pussy? Motherfucker, you'll be up there suckin' niggers' dicks.

DREXL

Heard that.

Drexl and Big D bump fists.

FLOYD

Yeah, that's right, laugh. It's so funny oh it's so funny.
(*he takes a hit off of a joint*)
There used to be a time when sisters didn't know shit about gettin' their pussy licked. Then the sixties came an' they started fuckin' around with white boys. And white boys are freaks for that shit –

DREXL

– Because it's good!

FLOYD

Then, after a while sisters get use to gettin' their little pussy eat. And because you white boys had to make pigs of yourselves, you fucked it up for every nigger in the world everywhere.

BIG D
(solemnly)
Drexl. On behalf of me and all the brothers who aren't here, I'd
like to express our gratitude –

Drexl and Big D bust up.

FLOYD
Go on, pussy-eaters . . . laugh. You look like you be eatin' pussy.
You got pussy-eatin' mugs. Now if a nigger wants to get his dick
sucked he's got to do a bunch of fucked-up shit.

BIG D
So you do eat pussy!

FLOYD
Naw naw!

BIG D
You don't like it but you eat that shit.
(to Drexl)
He eats it.

DREXL
Damn skippy. He like it, too.

BIG D
(mock English accent)
Me thinketh he doth protest too much.

FLOYD
Well fuck you guys, then! You guys are fucked up!

DREXL
Why you trippin'? We jus' fuckin' with ya. But I wanna ask you a
question. You with some fine bitch, I mean a brick shithouse bitch
– you're with Jayne Kennedy. You're with Jayne Kennedy and
you say, 'Bitch, suck my dick!' And then Jayne Kennedy says,
'First things first, nigger, I ain't suckin' shit till you bring your ass
over here an' lick my bush!' Now, what do you say?

FLOYD
I tell Jayne Kennedy, 'Suck my dick or I'll beat your ass!'

BIG D
Nigger, get real. You touch Jayne Kennedy she'll have you ass in Wayne County so fast –

DREXL
Nigger, back off, you ain't beatin' shit. Now what would you do?

FLOYD
I'd say fuck it!

Drexl and Big D get up from the table disgusted and walk away, leaving Floyd sitting all alone.

Big D sits on the bed, his back turned to Floyd, watching Bewitched.

FLOYD
(*yelling after them*)
Ain't no man have to eat pussy!

BIG D
(*not even looking*)
Take that shit somewhere else.

DREXL
(*marching back*)
You tell Jayne Kennedy to fuck it?

FLOYD
If it came down to who eats who, damn skippy.

DREXL
With that terrible mug of yours if Jayne Kennedy told you to eat her pussy, kiss her ass, lick her feet, chow on her shit, and suck her dogs dick, nigger, you'd aim to please.

BIG D
(*glued to TV*)
I'm hip.

DREXL
In fact, I'm gonna show you what I mean with a little demonstration. Big D, toss me that shotgun.

Without turning away from Bewitched *he picks up the shotgun and tosses it to Drexl.*

126

DREXL
(to Floyd)
All right, check this out.
(referring to shotgun)
Now, pretend this is Jayne Kennedy. And you're you.

Then, in a blink, he points the shotgun at Floyd and blows him away.

Big D leaps off the bed and spins toward Drexl.

Drexl, waiting for him, fires from across the room.

The blast hits the big man in the right arm and shoulder, spinning him around.

Drexl makes a beeline for his victim and fires again.

Big D is hit with a blast, full in the back. He slams into the wall and drops.

Drexl collects the suitcase full of cocaine and leaves. As he gets to the front door he surveys the carnage, spits, and walks out.

EXT. CLIFF'S MOVING CAR – MORNING

A big white Chevy Nova is driving down the road with a sunrise sky as a backdrop. The song 'Little Bitty Tear' is heard a cappella.

INT. CLIFF'S MOVING CAR – MORNING

Clifford Worley is driving his car home from work, singing this song gently to the sunrise. He's a forty-five-years-old ex-cop, at present a security guard. In between singing he takes sips from a cup of take-out coffee. He's dressed in a security guard uniform.

EXT. TRAILER PARK – MORNING

Cliff's Nova pulls in as he continues crooning. He pulls up to his trailer to see something that stops him short.

Cliff's POV through windshield.

Clarence and a nice-looking Young Woman are waiting for him in front of his trailer.

CU – Cliff

127

Upon seeing Clarence, a little bitty tear rolls down Cliff's cheek.

BACK TO: POV

Clarence and the Young Woman walk over to the car. Clarence sticks his face through the driver's side window.

> CLARENCE
>
> Good morning, Daddy. Long time no see.

INT. TRAILER HOME — MORNING

All three enter the trailer home.

> CLIFF
>
> Excuse the place, I haven't been entertaining company as of late. Sorry if I'm acting a little dense, but you're the last person in the world I expected to see this morning.

Clarence and the Young Girl walk into the living room.

> CLARENCE
>
> Yeah, well, tha's OK, Daddy, I tend to have that effect on people. I'm dyin' of thirst, you got anything to drink?

He moves past Cliff and heads straight for his refrigerator.

> CLIFF
>
> I think there's a Seven-Up in there.

> CLARENCE
> *(rumaging around the fridge)*
>
> Anything stronger?
> *(pause)*
> Oh, probably not. Beer? You can drink beer, can't you?

> CLIFF
>
> I can, but I don't.

> CLARENCE
> *(closing the fridge)*
>
> That's about all I ever eat.

Cliff looks at the girl. She smiles sweetly at him.

CLIFF
(*to girl*)
I'm sorry . . . I'm his father.

YOUNG GIRL
(*sticking her hand out*)
That's OK, I'm his wife.
(*shaking his hand vigorously*)
Alabama Worley, pleased to meetcha.

She is really pumping his arm, just like a used-car salesman. However, that's where the similarities end; Alabama's totally sincere.

Clarence steps back into the living room, holding a bunch of little ceramic fruit magnets in his hand. He throws his other arm around Alabama.

CLARENCE
Oh yeah, we got married.
(*referring to the magnets*)
You still have these!
(*to Alabama*)
This isn't a complete set; when I was five I swallowed the pomegranate one. I never shit it out, so I guess it's still there. Loverdoll, why don't you be a sport and go get us some beer. I want some beer.
(*to Cliff*)
Do you want some beer? Well, if you want some it's here.

He hands her some money and his car keys.

Go to the liquor store –
(*to Cliff*)
Where is there a liquor store around here?

CLIFF
Uh, yeah . . . there's a party store down 54th.

CLARENCE
(*to Alabama*)
Get a six-pack of something imported. It's hard to tell you what to get 'cause different places have different things. If they got Fosters, get that, if not ask the guy at the thing what the strongest imported beer he has is. Look, since you're making a beer run,

129

would you mind too terribly if you did a food run as well. I'm
fuckin' starvin' to death. Are you hungry too?

ALABAMA

I'm pretty hungry. When I went to the store I was gonna get some
Ding-Dongs.

CLARENCE

Well, fuck that shit, we'll get some real food. What would taste
good?

(to Cliff)

What do you think would taste good?

CLIFF

I'm really not very –

CLARENCE

You know what would taste good? Chicken. I haven't had chicken
in a while. Chicken would really hit the spot about now. Chicken
and beer, definitely, absolutely, without a doubt.

(to Cliff)

Where's a good chicken place around here?

CLIFF

I really don't know.

CLARENCE

You don't know the chicken places around where you live?

(to Alabama)

Ask the guy at the place where a chicken place is.

He gives her some more money.

This should cover it, Auggie-Doggie.

ALABAMA

Okee-dokee, Doggie-Daddy.

*She opens the door and starts out. Clarence turns to his dad as the door
shuts.*

CLARENCE

Isn't she the sweetest goddamned girl you ever saw in your whole
life? Is she a four alarm fire, or what?

130

CLIFF

She seems very nice.

CLARENCE

Daddy. Nice isn't the word. Nice is an insult. She's a peach.
That's the only word for it, she's a peach. She even tastes like a
peach. You can tell I'm in love with her. You can tell by my face,
can't ya? It's a dead giveaway. It's written all over it.

Ya know what? She loves me back. Take a seat, Pop, we gotta
talk –

CLIFF

Clarence, just shut up, you're giving me a headache! I can't
believe how much like your mother you are. You're your fucking
mother through and through. I haven't heard from ya in three
years. Then ya show up all of a sudden at eight o'clock in the
morning. You walk in like a goddamn bulldozer . . . don't get me
wrong, I'm happy to see you . . . just slow it down. Now, when
did you get married?

CLARENCE

Daddy, I'm in big fuckin' trouble and I really need your help.

BLACK TITLE CARD:

'HOLLYWOOD'

INT. OUTSIDE OF CASTING DIRECTOR'S OFFICE – DAY

*Four Young Actors are sitting on a couch with sheets of paper in their
hands silently mouthing lines. One of the actors is Dick Ritchie. The
casting director, Mary Louise Ravencroft, steps into the waiting room,
clipboard in hand.*

RAVENCROFT

Dick Ritchie?

Dick pops up from the pack.

DICK

I'm me . . . I mean, that's me.

RAVENCROFT

Step inside.

131

INT. CASTING DIRECTOR'S OFFICE — DAY

She sits behind a large desk. Her name-plate rests on the desktop. Several posters advertising The Return of T. J. Hooker *hang on the wall.*

Dick sits in a chair, holding his sheets in his hands.

RAVENCROFT

Well, the part you're reading for is one of the bad guys. There's Brian and Marty. Peter Breck's already been cast as Brian. And you're reading for the part of Marty. Now in this scene you're both in a car and Bill Shatner's hanging on the hood. And what you're trying to do is get him off.
(*she picks up a copy of the script*)
Whenever your ready.

DICK
(*reading and miming driving*)
Where'd he come from?

RAVENCROFT
(*reading from the script lifelessly*)
I don't know. He just appeared like magic.

DICK
(*reading from script*)
Well, don't just sit there, shoot him.

She puts her script down, and smiles at him.

RAVENCROFT
That was very good.

DICK
Thank you.

RAVENCROFT
If we decided on making him a New York type, could you do that?

DICK
Sure. No problem.

RAVENCROFT
Could we try it now?

DICK

Absolutely.

Dick picks up the script and begins, but this time with a Brooklyn accent.

Where'd he come from?

RAVENCROFT
(*monotone, as before*)

I don't know. He just appeared like magic.

DICK

Well, don't just sit there, shoot him.

Ravencroft puts her script down.

RAVENCROFT

Well, Mr Ritchie, I'm impressed. You're a very fine actor.

Dick smiles.

INT. TRAILER HOME – DAY

Cliff's completely aghast. He just stares, unable to come to grips with what Clarence has told him.

CLARENCE

Look, I know this is pretty heavy-duty, so if you wanna explode, feel free.

CLIFF

You're always makin' jokes. That's what you do, isn't it? Make jokes. Makin' jokes is the one thing you're good at, isn't it? But if you make a joke about this –
(*raising his voice*)
– I'm gonna go completely out of my fuckin' head!

Cliff pauses and collects himself.

What do you want from me?

CLARENCE

What?

133

CLIFF

Stop acting like an infant. You're here because you want me to
help you in some way. What do you need from me? You need
money?

CLARENCE

Do you still have friends on the force?

CLIFF

Yes, I still have friends on the force.

CLARENCE

Could you find out if they know anythin'? I don't think they
know shit about us. But I don't wanna *think*, I wanna *know*. You
could find out for sure what's goin' on.
                    (*pause*)
Daddy?

CLIFF

What makes you think I could do that?

CLARENCE

You were a cop.

CLIFF

What makes you think I would do that?

CLARENCE

I'm your son.

CLIFF

You got it all worked out, don't you?

CLARENCE

Look, goddamnit, I never asked you for a goddamn thing! I've
tried to make your parental obligation as easy as possible. After
Mom divorced you, did I ever ask you for anything? When I
wouldn't see ya for six months to a year at a time, did I ever get in
your shit about it? No! It was always: 'OK,' 'no problem,' 'you're
a busy guy, I understand.' The whole time you were a drunk, did
I ever point my finger at you and talk shit? No! Everybody else
did. I never did. You see, I know that you're just a bad parent.
You're not really very good at it. But I know you love me. I'm

134

basically a pretty resourceful guy. If I didn't really need it I wouldn't ask. And if you say no, don't worry about it. I'm gone. No problems.

Alabama walks in through the door carrying a shopping bag.

                         ALABAMA
The forager's back.

                         CLARENCE
Thank God. I could eat a horse if you slap enough catsup on it.

                         ALABAMA
I didn't get any chicken.

                         CLARENCE
How come?

                         ALABAMA
It's nine o'clock in the morning. Nothing's open.

INT. TRAILER HOME – BEDROOM – DAY

Cliff's on the telephone in his bedroom, pacing as he talks. The living room of the trailer can be seen from his doorway, where Clarence and Alabama are horsing around. They giggle and cut up throughout the scene. As Cliff talks, all the noise and hubbub of a police station comes through over the line. He's talking to Detective Wilson, an old friend of his from the force.

We see both sides of the conversation.

                         CLIFF
It's about that pimp that was shot a couple of days ago, Drexl Spivey.

                    DETECTIVE WILSON
What about him?

                         CLIFF
Well, Ted, to tell you the truth, I found out through the grapevine that it might be, and I only said *might* be, the Drexl Spivey that was responsible for that restaurant break-in on Riverdale.

WILSON

Are you still working security for Foster & Langley?

CLIFF

Yeah, and the restaurant's on my route. And you know I stuck my nose in for the company to try to put a stop to some of these break-ins. Now, while I have no proof, the name Drexl Spivey kept comin' up. Who's case is it?

WILSON

McTeague.

CLIFF

I don't know him. Is he a nice guy? You think he'll help me out?

WILSON

I don't see why not. When you gonna come round and see my new place?

CLIFF

You and Robin moved?

WILSON

Shit, you are behind. Me and Rob got a divorce six months ago. Got myself a new place – mirrors all over the bedroom, ceiling fans above the bed. Guy'd have to look as ugly as King Kong not to get laid in that place. I'm serious, a guy'd have to look like a gorilla.

CUT TO:

EXT. TRAILER HOME – DAY

Clarence and Cliff stand by Clarence's 1965 red Mustang. Alabama is amusing herself by doing cartwheels and handstands in the background.

CLIFF

They have nothing. In fact, they think it's drug related.

CLARENCE

Do tell. Why drug related?

CLIFF

Apparently, Drexl had his big toe stuck in shit like that.

136

CLARENCE

No shit?

CLIFF

Yeah. Drexl had an association with a fella named Blue Lou
Boyle. Name mean anything to you?

CLARENCE

Nope.

CLIFF

If you don't hang around his circle, no reason it should.

CLARENCE

Who is he?

CLIFF

Gangster. Drug dealer. Somebody you don't want on your ass.
Look, Clarence, the more I hear about this Drexl fucker, the more
I think you did the right thing. That guy wasn't just some wild
flake.

CLARENCE

That's what I've been tellin' ya. The guy was like a mad dog. So
the cops aren't lookin' for me?

CLIFF

Naw, until they hear something better they'll assume Drexl and
Blue Lou had a falling out. So, once you leave town I wouldn't
worry about it.

Clarence sticks his hand out to shake. Cliff takes it.

CLARENCE

Thanks a lot, Daddy. You really came through for me.

CLIFF

I got some money I can give you –

CLARENCE

Keep it.

CLIFF

Well, son, I want you to know I hope everything works out with
you and Alabama. I like her. I think you make a cute couple.

137

CLARENCE

We do make a cute couple, don't we?

CLIFF

Yeah, well, just stay outta trouble. Remember, you got a wife to think about now. Quit fuckin' around.

(*pause*)

I love you, son.

They hug each other.

Clarence takes a piece of paper out and puts it into Cliff's hand.

CLARENCE

This is Dick's number in Hollywood. We don't know where we'll be, but you can get a hold of me through him.

Clarence turns toward Alabama and yells to her.

Bama, we're outta here. Kiss Pops goodbye.

Alabama runs across from where she was and throws her arms around Cliff and gives him a big smackeroo on the lips. Cliff's a little startled. Alabama's bubbling like a Fresca.

ALABAMA

Bye, Daddy! Hope to see you again real soon.

CLARENCE

(*mock anger*)

What kind of daughterly smackeroo was that?

ALABAMA

Oh, hush up.

The two get into the Mustang.

CLARENCE

(*to Cliff*)

We'll send you a postcard as soon as we get to Hollywood.

Clarence starts the engine. The convertible roof opens as they talk.

CLIFF

Bama, you take care of that one for me. Keep him out of trouble.

ALABAMA

Don't worry, Daddy, I'm keepin' this fella on a short leash.

Clarence, slowly, starts driving away.

CLARENCE
(*to Cliff*)

As the sun sets slowly in the west we bid a fond farewell to all the friends we've made . . . and, with a touch of melancholy, we look forward to the time when we will all be together again.

Clarence peels out, shooting a shower of gravel up in the air.

As the Mustang disappears Cliff runs his tongue over his lips.

CLIFF

The son of a bitch was right . . . she does taste like a peach.

INT. DICK'S APARTMENT – DAY

Dick's apartment is standard issue for a young actor. Things are pretty neat and clean. A nice stereo unit sits on the shelf. A framed picture of a ballet dancer's feet hangs on the wall.

The phone rings, Dick answers.

DICK

Hi, Dick here.

INT. HOTEL SUITE – LAS VEGAS – SUNSET

Top floor, Las Vegas, Nevada hotel room with a huge picture window overlooking the neon-filled strip and the flaming red and orange sunset sky.

Clarence paces up and down with the telephone in his hand.

CLARENCE
(*big bopper voice*)

Heeeellllloooo baaaabbbbbyyyy!!

NOTE: *We intercut both sides of the conversation.*

DICK
(unsure)

Clarence?

CLARENCE

You got it.

DICK

It's great to hear from you.

CLARENCE

Well, you're gonna be seein' me shortly.

DICK

You comin' to LA? When?

CLARENCE

Tomorrow.

DICK

What's up? Why're ya leavin' Detroit?

Clarence sits down on the hotel room bed. Alabama, wearing only a long T-shirt with a big picture of Bullwinkle on it, crawls behind him.

CLARENCE

Well, there's a story behind all that. I'll tell you when I see you. By the way, I won't be alone. I'm bringin' my wife with me.

DICK

Get the fuck outta here!

CLARENCE

I'm a married man.

DICK

Get the fuck outta here!

CLARENCE

Believe it or not, I actually tricked a girl into falling in love with me. I'm not quite sure how I did it. I'd hate to have to do it again. But I did it. Wanna say hi to my better half?

Before Dick can respond Clarence puts Alabama on the phone.

140

ALABAMA

Hi, Dick. I'm Alabama Worley.

DICK

Hello, Alabama.

ALABAMA

I can't wait to meet you. Clarence told me all about you. He said you were his best friend. So, I guess that makes you my best friend, too.

Clarence starts dictating to her what to say.

CLARENCE

Tell him we gotta go.

ALABAMA

Clarence says we gotta be hittin' it.

DICK

What?

CLARENCE

Tell him we'll be hittin' his area some time tomorrow.

ALABAMA

He said don't go nowhere. We'll be there some time tomorrow.

DICK

Wait a minute –

CLARENCE

Tell him not to eat anything. We're gonna scarf when we get there.

ALABAMA

Don't eat anything.

DICK

Alabama, could you tell Clar –

CLARENCE

Ask him if he got the letter.

ALABAMA

Did you get the letter?

DICK

What letter?

ALABAMA
(*to Clarence*)

What letter?

CLARENCE

The letter I sent.

ALABAMA
(*to Dick*)

The letter he sent.

DICK

Clarence sent a letter?

CLARENCE

Has he gotten his mail today?

ALABAMA

Gotten your mail yet?

DICK

Yeah, my room-mate leaves it on the TV.

ALABAMA
(*to Clarence*)

Yes.

CLARENCE

Has he looked through it yet?

ALABAMA
(*to Dick*)

Ya looked through it?

DICK

Not yet.

ALABAMA
(*to Clarence*)

Nope.

142

CLARENCE

Tell him to look through it.

ALABAMA
(*to Dick*)

Get it.

DICK

Let me speak to Clarence.

ALABAMA
(*to Clarence*)

He wants to speak with you.

CLARENCE

No time. Gotta go. Just tell him to read the letter, the letter explains all. Tell him I love him. And tell him, as of tomorrow, all his money problems are over.

ALABAMA
(*to Dick*)

He can't. We gotta go, but he wants you to read the letter. The letter explains all. He wants you to know he loves you. And he wants you to know that as of tomorrow, all of your money problems are over.

DICK

Money problems?

CLARENCE

Now tell him goodbye.

ALABAMA

Bye, bye.

CLARENCE

Now hang up.

She hangs up the phone.

INT. DICK'S APARTMENT — DAY

Dick hears the click on the other end.

143

Hello, hello. Clarence? Clarence's wife? . . . I mean Alabama . . .
hello?

*Extremely confused. Dick hangs up the phone. He goes over to the TV
and picks up the day's mail. He goes through it.*

BILL: *Southern California Gas Company.*

BILL: *Group W.*

BILL: *Fossenkemp Photography.*

BILL: *Columbia Record and Tape Club.*

LETTER: *It's obviously from Clarence. Addressed to Dick. Dick opens it.*

EXT. TRAILER PARK — DAY

*A lower-middle-class trailer park named Astro World, which has a neon
sign in front of it in the shape of a planet.*

*A big, white Chevy Nova pulls into the park. It parks by a trailer that's
slightly less kept up than the others. Cliff gets out of the Chevy. He's
drinking out of a fast-food soda cup as he opens the door to his trailer.*

INT. TRAILER — DAY

*He steps inside his doorway and then, before he knows it, a gun is pressed
to his temple and a big hand grabs his shoulder.*

GUN CARRIER (DARIO)
Welcome home, alchy. We're havin' a party.

*Cliff is roughly shoved into his living room. Waiting for him are four
men, standing: Virgil, Frankie (young wise-guy), Lenny (an old wise-
guy), and Tooth-pick Vic (a fireplug pitbull type).*

*Sitting in Cliff's recliner is Vincenzo Coccotti, the Frank Nitti to Detroit
mob leader Blue Lou Boyle.*

*Cliff is knocked to his knees. He looks up and sees the sitting Coccotti.
Dario and Lenny pick him up and roughly drop him in a chair.*

COCCOTTI
(*to Frankie*)
Tell Tooth-pick Vic to go outside and do you-know-what.

In Italian Frankie tells Tooth-pick Vic what Coccotti said. He nods and exits.

Cliff's chair is moved closer to Coccotti's. Dario stands on one side of Cliff. Frankie and Lenny ransack the trailer. Virgil has a bottle of Chivas Regal in his hand, but he has yet to touch a drop.

Do you know who I am, Mr Worley?

CLIFF
I give up. Who are you?

COCCOTTI
I'm the Anti-Christ. You get me in a vendetta kind of mood, you will tell the angels in Heaven that you had never seen pure evil so singularly personified as you did in the face of the man who killed you. My name is Vincenzo Coccotti. I work as counsel for Mr Blue Lou Boyle, the man your son stole from. I hear you were once a cop so I can assume you've heard of us before. Am I correct?

CLIFF
I've heard of Blue Lou Boyle.

COCCOTTI
I'm glad. Hopefully that will clear up the how-full-of-shit-I-am question you've been asking yourself. Now, we're gonna have a little Q and A, and, at the risk of sounding redundant, please make your answers genuine.
(*taking out a pack of Chesterfields*)
Want a Chesterfield?

CLIFF
No.

COCCOTTI
(*as he lights one up*)
I have a son of my own. About your boy's age. I can imagine how painful this must be for you. But Clarence and that bitch-whore girlfriend of his brought this all on themselves. And I implore you

145

not to go down that road with 'em. You can always take comfort in
the fact that you never had a choice.

CLIFF

Look, I'd help ya if I could, but I haven't seen Clarence –

*Before Cliff can finish his sentence, Coccotti slams him hard in the nose
with his fist.*

COCCOTTI

Smarts, don't it? Gettin' slammed in the nose fucks you all up.
You got that pain shootin' through your brain. Your eyes fill up
with water. It ain't any kind a fun. But what I have to offer you,
that's as good as it's ever gonna get, and it won't ever get that good
again. We talked to your neighbors, they saw a Mustang, a red
Mustang, Clarence's red Mustang, parked in front of your trailer
yesterday. Mr Worley, have you seen your son?

Cliff's defeated.

CLIFF

I've seen him.

COCCOTTI

Now I can't be sure of how much of what he told you. So in the
chance you're in the dark about some of this, let me shed some
light. That whore your boy hangs around with, her pimp is an
associate of mine, and I don't just mean pimpin', in other affairs
he works for me in a courier capacity. Well, apparently, that dirty
little whore found out when we were gonna do some business,
'cause your son, the cowboy and his flame, came in the room
blastin' and didn't stop till they were pretty sure everybody was
dead.

CLIFF

What are you talkin' about?

COCCOTTI

I'm talkin' about a massacre. They snatched my narcotics and
hightailed it outta there. Wouldda gotten away with it, but your
son, fuckhead that he is, left his driver's license in a dead guy's
hand. A whore hiding in the commode filled in all the blanks.

146

CLIFF

I don't believe you.

COCCOTTI

That's of minor importance. But what's of major fuckin' importance is that I believe you. Where did they go?

CLIFF

On their honeymoon.

COCCOTTI

I'm gettin' angry askin' the same question a second time. Where did they go?

CLIFF

They didn't tell me.

Coccotti looks at him.

Now, wait a minute and listen. I haven't seen Clarence in three years. Yesterday he shows up here with a girl, sayin' he got married. He told me he needed some quick cash for a honeymoon, so he asked if he could borrow five hundred dollars. I wanted to help him out so I wrote out a check. We went to breakfast and that's the last I saw of him. So help me God.

They never thought to tell me where they were goin'. And I never thought to ask.

Coccotti looks at him for a long moment. He then gives Virgil a look. Virgil, quick as greased lightning, grabs Cliff's hand and turns it palm up. He then whips out a butterfly knife and slices Cliff's palm open and pours Chivas Regal on the wound. Cliff screams.

Coccotti puffs on a Chesterfield.

Tooth-pick Vic returns to the trailer, and reports in Italian that there's nothing in the car.

Virgil walks into the kitchen and gets a dishtowel. Cliff holds his bleeding palm in agony. Virgil hands him the dishtowel. Cliff uses it to wrap up his hand.

COCCOTTI

Sicilians are great liars. The best in the world. I'm a Sicilian. And my old man was the world heavyweight champion of Sicilian liars. And from growin' up with him I learned the pantomime. Now there are seventeen different things a guy can do when he lies to give him away. A guy has seventeen pantomimes. A woman's got twenty, but a guy's got seventeen. And if ya know 'em like ya know your own face, they beat lie detectors all to hell. What we got here is a little game of show and tell. You don't wanna show me nothing'. But you're tellin' me everything. Now I know you know where they are. So tell me, before I do some damage you won't walk away from.

The awful pain in Cliff's hand is being replaced by the awful pain in his heart. He looks deep into Coccotti's eyes.

CLIFF

Could I have one of those Chesterfields now?

COCCOTTI

Sure.

Coccotti leans over and hands him a smoke.

CLIFF

Got a match?

Cliff reaches into his pocket and pulls out a lighter.

Oh, don't bother. I got one.
                    (*he lights the cigarette*)
So you're a Sicilian, huh?

COCCOTTI
(*intensely*)

Uh-huh.

CLIFF

You know I read a lot. Especially things that have to do with history. I find that shit fascinating. In fact, I don't know if you know this or not, Sicilians were spawned by niggers.

All the men stop what they are doing and look at Cliff, except for Tooth-pick Vic, who doesn't speak English and so isn't insulted. Coccotti can't believe what he's hearing.

148

Come again?

It's a fact. Sicilians have nigger blood pumpin' through their hearts. If you don't believe me, look it up. You see, hundreds and hundreds of years ago the Moors conquered Sicily. And Moors are niggers. Way back then, Sicilians were like the wops in northern Italy. Blond hair, blue eyes. But, once the Moors moved in there, they changed the whole country. They did so much fuckin' with the Sicilian women, they changed the blood-line for ever, from blond hair and blue eyes to black hair and dark skin. I find it absolutely amazing to think that to this day, hundreds of years later, Sicilians still carry that nigger gene. I'm just quotin' history. It's a fact. It's written. Your ancestors were niggers. Your great, great, great, great, great-grandmother was fucked by a nigger, and had a half-nigger kid. That is a fact. Now tell me, am I lyin'?

Coccotti looks at him for a moment then jumps up, whips out an automatic, grabs hold of Cliff's hair, puts the barrel to his temple, and pumps three bullets through Cliff's head.

He pushes the body violently aside. Coccotti pauses. Unable to express his feelings and frustrated by the blood on his hands, he simply drops his weapon, and turns to his men.

COCCOTTI
I haven't killed anybody since 1974. Goddamn his soul to burn for eternity in fuckin' hell for makin' me spill blood on my hands! Go to this comedian's son's apartment and come back with somethin' that tells me where that asshole went so I can wipe this egg off of my face and fix this fucked-up family for good.

Tooth-pick Vic taps Frankie's shoulder and, in Italian, asks him what that was all about.

Lenny, who has been going through Cliff's refrigerator, has found a beer. When he closes the refrigerator door he finds a note held on by a ceramic banana magnet that says: 'Clarence in LA: Dick Ritchie (Number and address)'.

LENNY

Boss, get ready to get happy.

TITLE CARD:

'CLARENCE AND ALABAMA HIT LA'

INT. DICK'S APARTMENT – MORNING

Dick's asleep in a recliner. He's wearing his clothes from the night before. His room-mate Floyd is lying on the sofa watching TV.

The sound of four hands knocking on his door wakes Dick up. He shakes the bats out of his belfry, opens the door, and finds the cutest couple in Los Angeles standing in his doorway.

Clarence and Alabama immediately start singing 'Hello My Baby' like the frog in the old Chuck Jones cartoon.

CLARENCE/ALABAMA

Hello my baby,
Hello my honey,
Hello my ragtime gal –

DICK

Hi, guys.

Alabama throws her arms around Dick, and gives him a quick kiss. After she breaks, Clarence does the same. Clarence and Alabama walk right past Dick and into his apartment.

CLARENCE

Wow. Neat place.

INT. PINK'S HOT-DOG STAND – DAY

The Pink's employees work like skilled Benihana chefs as they assemble the ultimate masterpiece hot-dog.

EXT. PINK'S HOT-DOG STAND – PATIO – DAY

Clarence, Alabama, and Dick are sitting at an outdoor table chowing down on chili dogs. Alabama is in the middle of a story.

150

ALABAMA

. . . when my mom went into labor, my dad panicked. He never had a kid before, and crashed the car. Now, picture this: their car's demolished, crowd is starting to gather, my mom is yelling, going into contractions, and my dad, who was losing it before, is now completely screaming yellow zonkers. Then, out of nowhere, as if from thin air, this big giant bus appears, and the bus-driver says, 'Get her in here.' He forgot all about his route and just drove straight to the hospital. So, because he was such a nice guy, they wanted to name the baby after him, as a sign of gratitude. Well, his name was Waldo, and no matter how grateful they were, even if I'da been a boy, they wouldn't call me Waldo. So, they asked Waldo where he was from. And, so there you go.

CLARENCE

And here we are.

DICK

That's a pretty amazing story.

CLARENCE

Well, she's a pretty amazing girl. What are women like out here?

DICK

Just like in Detroit, only skinnier.

CLARENCE

You goin' out?

DICK

Well, for the past couple of years I've been goin' out with girls from my acting class.

CLARENCE

Good for you.

DICK

What's so fuckin' good about it? Actresses are the most fucked-in-the-head bunch of women in the world. It's like they gotta pass a test of emotional instability before they can get their SAG card. Oh, guess what? I had a really good reading for *T. J. Hooker* the other day.

151

ALABAMA

You're gonna be on *T. J. Hooker?*

DICK

Knock wood.

He knocks the table and then looks at it.

. . . formica. I did real well. I think she liked me.

CLARENCE

Did you meet Captain Kirk?

DICK

You don't meet him in the audition. That comes later. Hope, hope.

ALABAMA
(finishing her hot-dog)

That was so good I'm gonna have another.

DICK

You can't have just one.

Alabama leaves to get another hot-dog. Clarence never takes his eyes off her.

How much of that letter was on the up and up?

CLARENCE

Every word of it.

Dick sees where Clarence's attention is.

DICK

You're really in love, aren't you?

CLARENCE

For the very first time in my life.
(pause)
Do you know what that's like?

Clarence is so intense Dick doesn't know how to answer.

152

DICK
                    (*regretfully*)
No I don't.
                    (*he looks at Alabama*)
How did you two meet?

Clarence leans back thoughtfully and takes a sip from his Hebrew cream soda.

CLARENCE
Do you remember The Lyric?

INT. THE LYRIC THEATER — NIGHT

Sonny Chiba, as 'Streetfighter' Terry Surki, drives into a group of guys, fists and feet flying and whips ass on the silver screen.

Clarence sits, legs over the back of the chair in front of him, nibbling on popcorn, eyes big as saucers, and a big smile on his face.

EXT. THE LYRIC THEATER — NIGHT

A cab pulls up to the outside of The Lyric. The marquee carries the names of the triple feature: The Streetfighter, Return of the Streetfighter, *and* Sister Streetfighter. *Alabama steps out of the taxi cab and walks up to the box office.*

A box office girl reading comic looks at her.

ALABAMA
One please.

BOX OFFICE GIRL
Ninety-nine cents.

ALABAMA
Which one is on now?

BOX OFFICE GIRL
Return of the Streetfighter. It's been on about forty-five minutes.

INT. THE LYRIC THEATER – LOBBY – NIGHT

Alabama walks into the lobby and goes over to the concession stand. A young usher takes care of her.

ALABAMA

Can I have a medium popcorn? A super-large Mr Pibb, and a box of Goobers.

INT. THE LYRIC THEATER – NIGHT

It's still assholes and elbows on the screen with Sonny Chiba taking on all-comers.

Alabama walks through the doors with her bounty of food. She makes a quick scan of the theater. Not many people are there. She makes a beeline for the front which so happens to be Clarence's area of choice. She picks the row of seats just behind Clarence and starts asking her way down it.

Clarence turns and sees this beautiful girl all alone moving towards him. He turns his attention back to the screen, trying not to be so obvious.

When Alabama gets right behind Clarence, her foot thunks a discarded wine bottle, causing her to trip and spill her popcorn over Clarence.

ALABAMA

Oh, look what happened. Oh God, I'm so sorry. Are you OK?

CLARENCE

Yeah. I'm fine. It didn't hurt.

ALABAMA

I'm the clumsiest person in the world.

CLARENCE
(*picking popcorn out of his hair*)

It's OK. Don't worry about it. Accidents happen.

ALABAMA
(*picking popcorn out of his hair*)

What a wonderful philosophy. Thanks for being such a sweetheart. You could have been a real dick.

Alabama sits back in her seat to watch the movie.

154

Clarence tries to wipe her out of his mind, which isn't easy, and get back into the movie.

They both watch the screen for a moment. Then, Alabama leans forward and taps Clarence on the shoulder.

Excuse me . . . I hate to bother you again. Would you mind too terribly filling me in on what I missed?

Jumping at this opportunity.

CLARENCE

Not at all. OK, this guy here, he's Sonny Chiba.

ALABAMA

The oriental.

CLARENCE

The oriental in black. He's an assassin. Now, at the beginning he was hired to kill this guy the cops had. So he got himself arrested. They take him into the police station. And he starts kickin' all the cops' asses. Now, while keepin' them at bay, he finds the guy he was supposed to kill. Does a number on him. Kicks the cops' asses some more. Kicks the bars out of the window. And jumps out into a getaway car that was waiting for him.

ALABAMA

Want some Goobers?

CLARENCE

Thanks a lot.

ALABAMA

I thought Sonny was the good guy.

CLARENCE

He ain't so much good guy as he's just a bad motherfucker. Sonny don't be bullshittin'. He fucks dudes up for life. Hold on, a fight scene's comin' up.

They both watch, eyes wide, as Sonny Chiba kicks ass.

TIMECUT:

155

On the screen, Sonny Chiba's all jacked up. Dead bodies lie all around him. THE END (in Japanese) flashes on the screen.

The theater lights go up. Alabama's now sitting in the seat next to Clarence. They're both applauding.

                              ALABAMA
Great movie. Action-packed!

                              CLARENCE
Does Sonny kick ass or does Sonny kick ass?

                              ALABAMA
Sonny kicks ass.

                              CLARENCE
You shouldda saw the first original uncut version of the *Streetfighter*. It was the only movie up to that time rated X for violence. But we just saw the R.

                              ALABAMA
If that was the R, I'd love to see the X.

                              CLARENCE
My name is Clarence, and what is yours?

                              ALABAMA
Alabama Whitman. Pleased to meet ya.

                              CLARENCE
Is that your real name? Really?

                              ALABAMA
That's my real name, really. I got proof. See.

She shows Clarence her driver's license.

                              CLARENCE
Well, cut my legs off and call me Shorty. That's a pretty original moniker there, Alabama. Sounds like a Pam Grier movie.
                         (*announcer voice*)
She's a sixteen-calibre kitten, equally equipped for killin' an lovin'! She carried a sawed-off shotgun in her purse, a black belt around her waist, and the white-hot fire of hate in her eyes! Alabama Whitman is Pam Grier! Pray for forgiveness. Rated R . . . for Ruthless Revenge!

Clarence and Alabama are outside the theater. With the marquee lit up in the background they both perform unskilled martial arts moves. Clarence and Alabama break up laughing.

CLARENCE

Where's your car? I'll walk you to it.

ALABAMA

I took a cab.

CLARENCE

You took a cab to see three kung fu movies?

ALABAMA

Sure. Why not?

CLARENCE

Nothing. It's just you're a girl after my own heart.

ALABAMA

What time is it?

CLARENCE

'Bout twelve.

ALABAMA

I suppose you gotta get up early, huh?

CLARENCE

No. Not particularly.

(pause)

How come?

ALABAMA

Well, it's just when I see a really good movie I really like to go out and get some pie, and talk about it. It's sort of a tradition. Do you like to eat pie after you've seen a good movie?

CLARENCE

I love to get pie after a movie.

ALABAMA

Would you like to get some pie?

CLARENCE

I'd love some pie.

INT. DENNY'S RESTAURANT — NIGHT

Clarence and Alabama are sitting in a booth at an all-night Denny's. It's about 12:30 a.m. Clarence is having a piece of chocolate cream pie and a Coke. Alabama's nibbling on a piece of heated apple pie and sipping on a large Tab.

CLARENCE

Well, enough about the King. How about you?

ALABAMA

How 'bout me what?

CLARENCE

Tell me about yourself.

ALABAMA

There's nothing to tell.

CLARENCE

C'mon. What're ya tryin' to be? The Phantom Lady?

ALABAMA

What do you want to know?

CLARENCE

Well, for starters, what do you do? Where're ya from? What's your favorite color? Who's your favorite movie star? What kinda music do you like? What are your turn-ons and turn-offs? Do you have a fella? What's the story behind you takin' a cab to the most dangerous part of town alone? And, in a theater full of empty seats, why did you sit by me?

Alabama takes a bite of pie, puts down her fork, and looks at Clarence.

ALABAMA

Ask me them again. One by one.

CLARENCE

What do you do?

ALABAMA

I don't remember.

CLARENCE

Where are you from?

ALABAMA

I might be from Tallahassee. But I'm not sure yet.

CLARENCE

What's your favorite color?

ALABAMA

I don't remember. But off the top of my head, I'd say black.

CLARENCE

Who's your favorite movie star?

ALABAMA

Burt Reynolds.

CLARENCE

Would you like a bite of my pie?

ALABAMA

Yes, I would.

Clarence scoops up a piece on his fork and Alabama bites it off.

CLARENCE

Like it?

ALABAMA

Very much. Now, where were we?

CLARENCE

What kinda music do you like?

ALABAMA

Phil Spector. Girl group stuff. You know, like 'He's a Rebel.'

CLARENCE

What are your turn-ons?

ALABAMA

Mickey Rourke, somebody who can appreciate the finer things in life, like Elvis's voice, good kung fu, and a tasty piece of pie.

CLARENCE

Turn-offs?

ALABAMA

I'm sure there must be something, but I don't really remember.
The only thing that comes to mind are Persians.

CLARENCE

Do you have a fella?

She looks at Clarence and smiles.

ALABAMA

I'm not sure yet. Ask me again later.

CLARENCE

What's the story behind you takin' a cab to the most dangerous
part of town alone?

ALABAMA

Apparently, I was hit on the head with something really heavy,
giving me a form of amnesia. When I came to, I didn't know who I
was, where I was, or where I came from. Luckily, I had my
driver's license or I wouldn't even know my name. I hoped it
would tell me where I lived but it had a Tallahassee address on it,
and I stopped somebody on the street and they told me I was in
Detroit. So that was no help. But I did have some money on me,
so I hopped in a cab until I saw somethin' that looked familiar.
For some reason, and don't ask me why, that theater looked
familiar. So I told him to stop and I got out.

CLARENCE

And in a theater full of empty seats, why did you sit by me?

ALABAMA

Because you looked like a nice guy, and I was a little scared. And I
sure couldda used a nice guy about that time, so I spilled my
popcorn on you.

*Clarence looks at her closely. He picks up his soda and sucks on the straw
until it makes that slurping sound. He puts it aside and stares into her
soul.*

160

A smile cracks on her face and develops into a big wide grin.

Aren't you just dazzled by my imagination, lover boy?
(*eats her last piece of pie*)
Where to next?

INT. COMIC BOOK STORE – NIGHT

It's about 1:30 a.m. Clarence has taken Alabama to where he works. It's a comic book store called Heroes For Sale. Alabama thinks this place is super-cool.

ALABAMA
Wow. What a swell place to work.

CLARENCE
Yeah, I got the key, so I come here at night, hang out, read comic books, play music.

ALABAMA
How long have you worked here?

CLARENCE
Almost four years.

ALABAMA
That's a long time.

CLARENCE
I'm hip. But you know, I'm comfortable here. It's easy work. I know what I'm doing. Everybody who works here is my buddy. I'm friendly with most of the customers. I just hang around and talk about comic books all day.

ALABAMA
Do you get paid a lot?

CLARENCE
That's where trouble comes into paradise. But the boss let's you borrow money if you need it. Wanna see what *Spiderman* number one looks like?

ALABAMA
You bet. How much is that worth?

161

Clarence gets a box off the shelf.

CLARENCE

Four hundred bucks.

ALABAMA

I didn't even know they had stores that just sold comic books.

CLARENCE

Well, we sell other things too. Cool stuff. *Man from U.N.C.L.E.*
lunch boxes. *Green Hornet* board games. Shit like that. But comic
books are our main business. There's a lot of collectors around
here.

She holds up a little GI Joe sized action figure of a black policeman.

ALABAMA

What's that?

CLARENCE

That's a *Rookies* doll. George Sanford Brown. We gotta lotta dolls.
They're real cool. Did you know they came out with dolls for all
the actors in *The Black Hole*? I always found it funny that
somewhere there's a kid playin' with a little figure of Ernest
Borgnine.

He pulls out a plastic-encased Spiderman *comic from the box.*

Spiderman, number one. The one that started it all.

Clarence shows the comic book to Alabama.

ALABAMA

God, Spiderman looks different.

CLARENCE

He was just born, remember? This is the first one. You know that
guy, Dr Gene Scott? He said that the story of Spiderman is the
story of Christ, just disguised. Well, I thought about that even
before I heard him say it. Hold on, let me show you my favorite
comic book cover of all time.

He pulls out another comic

Sgt Fury and His Howling Commandos. One of the coolest series
known to man. They're completely worthless. You can get

162

number one for about four bucks. But that's one of the cool things about them, they're so cheap.
(*he opens one up*)
Just look at that artwork, will ya. Great stories. Great characters. Look at this one.

We see the Sgt Fury *panels.*

Nick's gotten a ring for his sweetheart and he wears it around his neck on a chain. OK, later in the story he gets into a fight with a Nazi bastard on a ship. He knocks the guy overboard, but the Kraut grabs ahold of his chain and the ring goes overboard too. So, Nick dives into the ocean to get it. Isn't that cool?

She's looking into Clarence's eyes. He turns and meets her gaze.

Alabama, I'd like you to have this.

Clarence hands her the Sgt Fury and His Howling Commandos *comic book that he loves so much.*

INT. CLARENCE'S APARTMENT — BEDROOM — NIGHT

Clarence's bedroom is a pop culture explosion. Movie posters, pictures of Elvis, anything you can imagine. The two walk through the door.

ALABAMA
What a cool room!

She runs and does a jumping somersault into his bed.

Later. Alabama's sitting Indian-style going through Clarence's photo album. Clarence is behind her planting little kisses on her neck and shoulders.

Oooooh, you look so cute in your little cowboy outfit. How old were you then?

CLARENCE
Five.

She turns the page.

ALABAMA
Oh, you looked so cute as a little Elvis.

CLARENCE

I finally knew what I wanted to be when I grew up.

LATER — LIVING ROOM

Clarence and Alabama slow dance in the middle of his room to Janis Joplin's 'Piece of My Heart.'

CLARENCE

You know when you sat behind me?

ALABAMA

At the movies?

CLARENCE

Uh-huh, I was tryin' to think of somethin' to say to you, then I thought, she doesn't want me bothering her.

ALABAMA

What would make you think that?

CLARENCE

I dunno. I guess I'm just stupid.

ALABAMA

You're not stupid. Just wrong.

They move to the music. Alabama softly, quietly sings some of the words to the song.

I love Janis.

CLARENCE

You know, a lot of people have misconceptions of how she died.

ALABAMA

She OD'd, didn't she?

CLARENCE

Yeah, she OD'd. But she wasn't on her last legs or anythin'. She didn't take too much. It shouldn't have killed her. There was somethin' wrong with what she took.

ALABAMA

You mean she got a bad batch?

CLARENCE

That's what happened. In fact, when she died, it was considered
to be the happiest time of her life. She'd been fucked over so much
by men she didn't trust them. She was havin' this relationship
with this guy and he asked her to marry him. Now, other people
had asked to marry her before, but she couldn't be sure whether
they really loved her or were just after her money. So, she said no.
And the guy says, 'Look, I really love you, and I wanna prove it.
So have your lawyers draw up a paper that says no matter what
happens, I can never get any of your money, and I'll sign it.' So
she did, and he did, and he asked her, and she said yes. And once
they were engaged he told her a secret about himself that she never
knew; he was a millionaire.

ALABAMA

So he really loved her?

CLARENCE

Uh-huh.

They kiss.

INT. CLARENCE'S APARTMENT – BEDROOM – DAY

*It's the next day, around 1 p.m. Clarence wakes up in his bed, alone. He
looks around, and no Alabama. Then he hears crying in the distance. He
puts on a robe and investigates.*

INT. CLARENCE'S APARTMENT – LIVING ROOM – DAY

*Alabama's wearing one of Clarence's old shirts. She's curled up in a chair
crying. Clarence approaches her. She tries to compose herself.*

CLARENCE

What's wrong, sweetheart? Did I do something? What did I do?

ALABAMA

You didn't do nothing.

CLARENCE

Did you hurt yourself?

165

(he takes her foot)
Whatd'ya do? Step on a thumbtack?

ALABAMA
Clarence, I've got something to tell you. I didn't just happen to be at that theater. I was paid to be there.

CLARENCE
What are you, a theater checker? You check up on the box office girls. Make sure they're not rippin' the place off.

ALABAMA
I'm not a theater checker. I'm a call girl.

Pause.

CLARENCE
You're a whore?

ALABAMA
I'm a call girl. There's a difference, ya know.
(pause)
I don't know. Maybe there's not. That place you took me to last night, that comic book place.

CLARENCE
Heroes For Sale?

ALABAMA
Yeah, that one. Somebody who works there arranged to have me meet you.

CLARENCE
Who?

ALABAMA
I don't know, I didn't talk with them. The plan was for me to bump into you, pick you up, spend the night, and skip out after you fell asleep. I was gonna write you a note and say that this was my last day in America. That I was leaving on a plane this morning to the Ukraine to marry a rich millionaire, and thank you for making my last day in America my best day.

166

CLARENCE

That dazzling imagination.

ALABAMA

It's over on the TV. All it says is: Dear Clarence. I couldn't write anymore. I didn't not want to ever see you again. In fact, it's stupid not to ever see you again. Last night . . . I don't know . . . I felt . . . I hadn't had that much fun since Girl Scouts. So I just said, 'Alabama, come clean. Let him know what's what, and if he tells you to go fuck yourself then go back to Drexl and fuck yourself.'

CLARENCE

Who and what is a Drexl?

ALABAMA

My pimp.

CLARENCE

You have a pimp?

ALABAMA

Uh-huh.

CLARENCE

A real live pimp?

ALABAMA

Uh-huh.

CLARENCE

Is he black?

ALABAMA

He thinks he is. He says his mother was Apache, but I suspect he's lying.

CLARENCE

Is he nice?

ALABAMA

Well, I wouldn't go so far as to call him nice, but he's treated me pretty decent. But I've only been there about four days. He got a little rough with Arlene the other day.

167

CLARENCE

What did he do to Arlene?

ALABAMA

Slapped her around a little. Punched her in the stomach. It was
pretty scary.

CLARENCE

This motherfucker sounds charming!

Clarence is on his feet, furious.

Goddamn it, Alabama, you gotta get the fuck outta there! How
much longer before he's slappin' you around? Punchin' you in the
stomach? How the fuck did you get hooked up with a douche-bag
like this in the first place?

ALABAMA

As the bus station. He said I'd be a perfect call girl. And that he
knew an agency in California that, on his recommendation, would
handle me. They have a very exclusive clientele: movie stars, big
businessmen, total white-collar. And all the girls in the agency get
a grand a night. At least five hundred. They drive Porsches, live in
condos, have stockbrokers, carry beepers, you know, like Nancy
Allen in *Dressed to Kill*. And when I was ready he'd call 'em, give
me a plane ticket, and send me on my way. He says he makes a
nice finder's fee for finding them hot prospects. But no one's
gonna pay a grand a night for a girl who doesn't know whether to
shit or wind her watch. So what I'm doin' for Drexl now is just
sorta learnin' the ropes. It seemed like a lotta fun, but I don't
really like it much, till last night. You were only my third trick,
but you didn't feel like a trick. Since it was a secret, I just
pretended I was on a date. And, um, I guess I want a second date.

CLARENCE

Thank you. I wanna see you again too. And again, and again, and
again. Bama, I know we haven't known each other long, but my
parents went together all throughout high school, and they still
got a divorce. So, fuck it, you wanna marry me?

ALABAMA

What?

168

CLARENCE
Will you be my wife?

When Alabama gives her answer, her voice cracks.

ALABAMA
Yes.

CLARENCE
(a little surprised)
You will?

ALABAMA
You better not be fucking teasing me.

CLARENCE
You better not be fuckin' teasin' me.

They seal it with a kiss.

LATER — THAT NIGHT

CU – Alabama's wedding ring.

The newlyweds are snuggling up together on the couch watching TV. The movie they're watching is The Incredible One-Armed Boxer vs. the Master of the Flying Guillotine. *Alabama watches the screen, but every so often she looks down to admire the ring on her hand.*

CLARENCE
Did ya ever see *The Chinese Professionals?*

ALABAMA
I don't believe so.

CLARENCE
Well, that's the one that explains how Jimmy Wang Yu became the Incredible One-Armed Boxer.

We hear, off screen, the TV Announcer say:

TV ANNOUNCER
(off)
We'll return to Jimmy Wang Yu in . . . *The Incredible One-Armed Boxer vs. the Master of the Flying Guillotine,* tonight's eight o'clock

169

movie, after these important messages . . .

Clarence looks at the TV. He feels the warmth of Alabama's hand holding his. We see commercials playing.

He turns in her direction. She's absent-mindedly looking at her wedding ring.

He smiles and turns back to the TV.

More commercials.

Dolly close on Clarence's face.

FLASH ON:

Alabama, right after he proposed.

> ALABAMA
> You better not be fucking teasing me.

FLASH ON:

In a cute, all-night wedding chapel. Clarence dressed in a rented tuxedo and Alabama in a rented white wedding gown.

> ALABAMA
> I do.

> CLARENCE
> Thank you.

FLASH ON:

Clarence and Alabama, dressed in tux and gown, doing a lovers' waltz on a ballroom dance floor.

FLASH ON:

Clarence and Alabama in a taxi cab.

> CLARENCE
> Hello, Mrs Worley.

> ALABAMA
> How do you do, Mr Worley?

> CLARENCE
> Top o' the morning to you, Mrs Worley.

170

ALABAMA
Bottom of the ninth. Mr Worley. Oh, by the by, Mr Worley, have you seen your lovely wife today?

CLARENCE
Oh, you're speaking of my charming wife Mrs Alabama Worley.

ALABAMA
Of course. Are there others, Mr Worley?

Moving on top of her.

CLARENCE
Not for me.

He starts kissing her and moving her down on the seat. She resists.

ALABAMA
(*playfully*)
No no no no no no no no no . . .

CLARENCE
(*playfully*)
Yes yes yes yes yes yes yes yes . . .

FLASH ON:

A big mean-looking black man in pimp's clothes.

PIMP
Bitch, you better git yo ass back on the street an' git me my money!

FLASH ON:

Pimp on street corner with his arm around Alabama, giving a sales pitch to a potential customer.

PIMP
I'm tellin' you, my man, this bitch is fine. This girl's a freak! You can fuck 'er in the ass, fuck 'er in the mouth. Rough stuff, too. She's a freak for it. Jus' try not to fuck 'er up for life.

FLASH ON:

Pimp beating Alabama.

PIMP

You holdin' out on me, girl? Bitch, you never learn!

FLASH ON:

Alabama passionately kissing the uninterested pimp.

PIMP

Hang it up, momma. I got no time for this bullshit.

BACK TO:

TV showing kung fu film.

Back to Clarence's face. There's definitely something different about his eyes.

Clarence springs off the couch and goes into his bedroom. Alabama's startled by his sudden movement.

ALABAMA
(*yelling after him*)

Where you goin', honey?

CLARENCE
(*off*)

I just gotta get somethin'.

INT. CLARENCE'S APARTMENT — BATHROOM — NIGHT

Clarence splashes water on his face, trying to wash away the images that keep polluting his mind. Then, he hears a familiar voice.

FAMILIAR VOICE
(*off*)

Well? Can you live with it?

Clarence turns and sees that the voice belongs to Elvis Presley. Clarence isn't surprised to see him.

CLARENCE

What?

ELVIS

Can you live with it?

172

CLARENCE
Live with what?

ELVIS

With that son of a bitch walkin' around breathin' the same air as
you? And gettin' away with it every day. Are you haunted?

CLARENCE

Yeah.

ELVIS

You wanna get unhaunted?

CLARENCE

Yeah.

ELVIS

Then shoot 'em. Shoot 'em in the face. And feed that boy to the dogs.

CLARENCE

I can't believe what the fuck you're tellin' me.

ELVIS

I ain't tellin' ya nothin'. I'm just sayin' what I'd do.

CLARENCE

You'd really do that?

ELVIS

He don't got no right to live.

CLARENCE

Look, Elvis, he is hauntin' me. He doesn't deserve to live. And I do
want to kill him. But I don't wanna go to jail for the rest of my life.

ELVIS

I don't blame you.

CLARENCE

If I thought I could get away with it –

ELVIS

Killin' 'em's the hard part. Gettin' away with it's the easy part.
Whaddya think the cops do when a pimp's killed? Burn the
midnight oil tryin' to find who done it? They couldn't give a flyin'

173

fuck if all the pimps in the whole wide world took two in the back of
the fuckin' head. If you don't get caught at the scene with the
smokin' gun in your hand, you got away with it.

Clarence looks at Elvis.

Clarence, I like ya. Always have, always will.

INT. CLARENCE'S APARTMENT – BEDROOM – NIGHT

*CU – A snub-nosed .38, which Clarence loads and sticks down his heavy
athletic sock.*

INT. CLARENCE'S APARTMENT – LIVING ROOM – NIGHT

Clarence returns.

> CLARENCE
> Sweetheart, write down your former address.

> ALABAMA
> What?

> CLARENCE
> Write down Drexl's address.

> ALABAMA
> Why?

> CLARENCE
> So I can go over there and pick up your things.

> ALABAMA
> *(really scared)*
> No, Clarence. Just forget it, babe. I just wanna disappear from there.

He kneels down before her and holds her hand.

> CLARENCE
> Look, sweetheart, he scares you. But I'm not scared of that
> motherfucker. He can't touch you now. You're completely out of
> his reach. He poses absolutely no threat to us. So, if he doesn't
> matter, which he doesn't, it would be stupid to lose your things,
> now wouldn't it.

174

ALABAMA
You don't know him –

CLARENCE
You don't know me. Not when it comes to shit like this. I have to do this. I need for you to know you can count on me to protect you. Now write down the address.

TITLE CARD:

'CASS QUARTER, HEART OF DETROIT'

EXT. DOWNTOWN DETROIT STREET – NIGHT

It's pretty late at night. Clarence steps out of his red Mustang. He's right smack dab in the middle of a bad place to be in the daytime. He checks the pulse on his neck; it's beating like a race horse. To pump himself up he does a quick Elvis Presley gyration.

CLARENCE
(*in Elvis voice*)
Yeah . . . yeah . . .

He makes a beeline for the front door of a large, dark apartment building.

INT. DARK BUILDING – NIGHT

He's inside. His heart's really racing now. He has the TV guide that Alabama wrote the address on in his hand. He climbs a flight of stairs and makes his way down a dark hallway to apartment 22, the residence of Drexl Spivey. Clarence knocks on the door.

A Young Black Man, about twenty years old, answers the door. He has really big biceps and is wearing a black and white fishnet football jersey.

YOUNG BLACK MAN
You want somethin'?

CLARENCE
Drexl?

Naw, man, I'm Marty. Whatcha want?

CLARENCE

I gotta talk to Drexl.

MARTY

Well, what the fuck you wanna tell him?

CLARENCE

It's about Alabama.

A figure jumps in the doorway wearing a yellow Farah Fawcett T-shirt. It's our friend, Drexl Spivey.

DREXL

Where the fuck is that bitch?

CLARENCE

She's with me.

DREXL

Who the fuck are you?

CLARENCE

I'm her husband.

DREXL

Well. That makes us practically related. Bring your ass on in.

INT. DREXL'S LIVING ROOM – NIGHT

Drexl and Marty about-face and walk into the room, continuing a conversation they were having and leaving Clarence standing in the doorway. This is not the confrontation Clarence expected. He trails in behind Drexl and Marty.

DREXL
(*to Marty*)

What was I sayin'?

MARTY

Rock whores.

DREXL

You ain't seen nothin' like these rock whores. They ass be young man. They got that fine young pussy. Bitches want the rock they be a freak for you. They give you hips, lips, and fingertips.

Drexl looks over his shoulder at Clarence.

(*to Clarence*)
You know what I'm talkin' about.

Drexl gestures to one of the three stoned Hookers lounging about the apartment.

(*to Marty*)
These bitches over here ain't shit. You stomp them bitches to death to get to the kind of pussy I'm talkin' about.

Drexl sits down at a couch with a card table in front of it, scattered with take-out boxes of Chinese food. A black exploitation movie is playing on TV.

Looky here, you want the bitches to really fly high, make your rocks with Cherry Seven-Up.

MARTY

Pussy love pink rocks.

This is not how Clarence expected to confront Drexl, but this is exactly what he expected Drexl to be like. He positions himself in front of the food table, demanding Drexl's attention.

DREXL
(*eating with chopsticks, to Clarence*)
Grab a seat there, boy. Want some dinner? Grab yourself an egg roll. We got everything here from a diddle-eyed-Joe to a damned-if-I-know.

CLARENCE

No thanks.

DREXL

No thanks? What does that mean? Means you ate before you came on down here? All full. Is that it? Naw, I don't think so. I think you're too scared to be eatin'. Now, see we're sittin' down here,

177

ready to negotiate, and you've already given up your shit. I'm still a mystery to you. But I know exactly where your ass is comin' from.

See, if I asked you if you wanted some dinner and you grabbed an egg roll and started to chow down, I'd say to myself, 'This motherfucker's carryin' on like he ain't got a care in the world. Who knows? Maybe he don't. Maybe this fool's such a bad motherfucker, he don't got to worry about nothin', he just sit down, eat my Chinese, watch my TV.' See? You ain't even sat down yet. On that TV there, since you been in the room, is a woman with her titties hangin' out, and you ain't even bothered to look. You just been starin' at me. Now, I know I'm pretty, but I ain't as pretty as a couple of titties.

Clarence takes out an envelope and throws it on the table.

CLARENCE

I'm not eatin' cause I'm not hungry. I'm not sittin' 'cause I'm not stayin'. I'm not lookin' at the movie 'cause I saw it seven years ago. It's *The Mack* with Max Julian, Carol Speed, and Richard Pryor, written by Bobby Poole, directed by Michael Campus, and released by Cinerama Releasing Company in 1984. I'm not scared of you. I just don't like you. In that envelope is some payoff money. Alabama's moving on to some greener pastures. We're not negotiatin'. I don't like to barter. I don't like to dicker. I never have fun in Tijuana. That price is non-negotiable. What's in that envelope is for my peace of mind. My peace of mind is worth that much. Not one penny more, not one penny more.

You could hear a pin drop. Once Clarence starts talking Marty goes on full alert. Drexl stops eating and the Whores stop breathing. All eyes are on Drexl. Drexl drops his chopsticks and opens the envelope. It's empty.

DREXL

It's empty.

Clarence flashes a wide Cheshire cat grin that says, 'That's right, asshole.'

Silence.

178

Oooooooooh weeeeeeee! This child is terrible. Marty, you know what we got here? Motherfuckin' Charles Bronson. Is that who you supposed to be? Mr Majestyk? Looky here, Charlie, none of this shit is necessary. I ain't got no hold on Alabama. I just tryin' to lend the girl a helpin' hand –

Before Drexl finishes his sentence he picks up the card table and throws it at Clarence, catching him off guard.

Marty comes up behind Clarence and throws his arm around his neck, putting him in a tight choke hold.

Clarence, with his free arm, hits Marty hard with his elbow in the solar plexus. We'll never know if that blow had any effect because at just that moment Drexl takes a flying leap and tackles the two guys.

All of them go crashing into the stereo unit and a couple of shelves that hold records, all of which collapse to the floor in a shower of LPs.

Marty, who's on the bottom of the pile, hasn't let go of Clarence.

Since Drexl's on top, he starts slamming his fists into Clarence's face.

Clarence, who's sandwiched between these two guys, can't do a whole lot about it.

Ya wanna fuck wit me?
> *(hits Clarence)*

Ya wanna fuck wit me?
> *(hits Clarence)*

I'll show ya who you're fuckin' wit!

He hits Clarence hard in the face with both fists.

Clarence, who has no leverage whatsoever, grabs hold of Drexl's face and digs his nails in. He sticks his thumb in Drexl's mouth, grabs a piece of cheek, and starts twisting.

Marty, who's in an even worse position, can do nothing but tighten his grip around Clarence's neck, until Clarence feels like his eyes are going to pop out of his head.

Drexl's face is getting torn up, but he's also biting down hard on Clarence's thumb.

179

Clarence raises his head and brings it down fast, crunching Marty's face, and busting his nose.

Marty loosens his grip around Clarence's neck. Clarence wiggles free and gets up on to his knees.

Drexl and Clarence are now on an even but awkward footing. The two are going at each other like a pair of alley cats, not aiming their punches, just keeping them coming fast and furious. They're not doing much damage to each other because of their positions, it's almost like a hockey fight.

Marty sneaks up behind Clarence and smashes him in the head with a stack of LPs. This disorients Clarence. Marty grabs him from behind and pulls him to his feet.

Drexl socks him in the face: one, two, three! Then he kicks him hard in the balls.

Marty lets go and Clarence hits the ground like a sack of potatoes. He curls up into a fetal position and holds his balls, tears coming out of his eyes.

Drexl's face is torn up from Clarence's nails.

Marty has blood streaming down his face from his nose and on to his shirt.

(*to Marty*)
You OK? That stupid dumb-ass didn't break your nose, did he?

MARTY
Naw. It don't feel too good but it's all right.

Drexl kicks Clarence, who's still on the ground hurting.

DREXL
(*to Clarence*)
You see what you get when you fuck wit me, white boy? You're gonna walk in my goddamn house, my house! Gonna come in here and tell me! Talkin' that smack, in my house, in front of my employees. Shit! Your ass must be crazy.
(*to Marty*)
I don't think this white boy's got good sense. Hey, Marty.

180

(laughing)
He must of thought it was white boy day. It ain't white boy day, is
it?

MARTY
(laughing)
Naw, man, it ain't white boy day.

DREXL
(to Clarence)
Shit, man, you done fucked up again. Next time you bogart your
way into a nigger's crib, an' get all in his face, make sure you do it
on white boy day.

CLARENCE
(hurting)
Wannabee nigger . . .

DREXL
Fuck you! My mother was Apache.

Drexl kicks him again. Clarence curls up.

Drexl bends down and looks for Clarence's wallet in his jacket.

Clarence still can't do much. The kick to his balls still has him down.

Drexl finds it and pulls it out. He flips it open to the driver's license.

Well, well, well, looky what we got here. Clarence Worley.
Sounds almost like a nigger name.
(to Clarence)
Hey, dummy.

He puts his foot on Clarence's chest. Clarence's POV, as he looks up.

Before you brought your dumb ass through the door, I didn't
know shit. I just chalked it up to au revoir Alabama. But, because
you think you're some macho motherfucker, I know who she's
with. You. I know who you are, Clarence Worley. And, I know
where you live, 4900 116th Street, apartment 48. And I'll make a
million-dollar bet, Alabama's at the same address. Marty, take the
car and go get 'er. Bring her dumb ass back here.

He hands Marty the driver's license. Marty goes to get the car keys and a jacket.

> (*to Marty*)
> I'll keep lover boy here entertained.
> (*to Clarence*)
> You know the first thing I think I'll do when she gets here. I think I'll make her suck my dick, and I'll come all in her face. I mean it ain't nuttin' new. She's done it before. But I want you as a audience.
> (*hollering to Marty*)
> Marty, what the fuck are you doin'?

MARTY
(*off*)

I'm tryin' to find my jacket.

DREXL

Look in the hamper. Linda's been dumpin' everybody's stray clothes there lately.

While Drexl has his attention turned to Marty, Clarence reaches into his sock and pulls out the .38. He stick the barrel between Drexl's legs. Drexl, who's standing over Clarence, looks down just in time to see Clarence pull the trigger and blow his balls to bits. Tiny spots of blood speckle Clarence's face.

Drexl shrieks in horror and pain, and falls to the ground.

MARTY
(*off*)

What's happening?

Marty steps into the room.

Clarence doesn't hesitate, he shoots Marty four times in the chest.

Two of the three Hookers have run out of the front door, screaming. The other Hooker is curled up in the corner. She's too stoned to run, but stoned enough to be terrified.

Drexl, still alive, is laying on the ground howling, holding what's left of his balls and dick.

Clarence points the gun at the remaining Hooker.

> CLARENCE
> Get a bag and put Alabama's things in it!

She doesn't move.

> You wanna get shot? I ain't got all fuckin' day, so move it!

The Hooker, tears of fear ruining her mascara, grabs a suitcase from under the bed, and, on her hands and knees, pushes it along the floor to Clarence.

Clarence takes it by the handle and wobbles over to Drexl, who's curled up like a pillbug.

CU – *Clarence's forgotten driver's license in Marty's bloody hand.*

Clarence puts his foot on Drexl's chest.

> (*to Drexl*)
> Open your eyes, laughing boy.

He doesn't. Clarence gives him a kick.

> Open your eyes!

He does. It's now Drexl's POV from on the floor.

> You thought it was pretty funny, didn't you?

He fires.

CU – *the bullet comes out of the gun and heads right toward us. When it reaches us, the screen goes awash in red.*

INT. CLARENCE'S APARTMENT – NIGHT

The front door swings open and Clarence walks in. Alabama jumps off the couch and runs toward Clarence, before she reaches him he blurts out:

> CLARENCE
> I killed him.

She stops short.

> I've got some food in the car, I'll be right back.

Clarence leaves. Except for the TV playing, the room is quiet. Alabama sits on the couch.

Clarence walks back into the room with a whole bounty of take-out food. He heaps it on to the coffee table and starts to chow down.

Help yourself. I got enough. I am fuckin' starvin'. I think I ordered one of everythin'.

He stops and looks at her.

I am so hungry.

He starts eating french fries and hamburgers.

> ALABAMA
> (*in a daze*)

Was it him or you?

> CLARENCE

Yeah. But to be honest, I put myself in that position. When I drove up there I said to myself, 'If I can kill 'em and get away with it, I'll do it.' I could. So I did.

> ALABAMA

Is this a joke?

> CLARENCE

No joke. This is probably the best hamburger I've ever had. I'm serious, I've never had a hamburger taste this good.

Alabama starts to cry. Clarence continues eating, ignoring her.

Come on, Bama, eat something. You'll feel better.

She continues crying. He continues eating and ignoring her. Finally he spins on her, yelling:

Why are you crying? He's not worth one of your tears. Would you rather it had been me? Do you love him?
> (*no answer*)

Do you love him?
> (*no answer*)

Do you love him?

She looks at Clarence, having a hard time getting a word out.

184

ALABAMA

I think what you did was . . .

CLARENCE

What?

ALABAMA

I think what you did . . .

CLARENCE

What?

ALABAMA

I think what you did . . .

CLARENCE

What?

ALABAMA

. . . was so romantic.

Clarence is completely taken aback. They meet in a long, passionate lovers' kiss. Their kiss breaks and slowly the world comes back to normal.

I gotta get outta these clothes.

CLARENCE

I have your things right here.

He picks up the suitcase and drops it on the table in front of them.

ALABAMA
(*comically*)

Clean clothes. There is a God.

Clarence flips open the suitcase. Alabama's and her husband's jaws drop.

Clarence. Those aren't my clothes.

CUT TO:

EXT. HOLLYWOOD HOLIDAY INN – DAY

We see the Hollywood Holiday Inn sign. Pan to the parking lot where Clarence's empty red Mustang is parked.

185

CU — Dick's jaw drops. His hand reaches out of shot.

CU — The reason for all the jaw dropping . . . the suitcase is full of cocaine! Dick's hand enters frame and fondles a bag.

Clarence smiles, holding a bottle of wine.

Alabama's watching the cable TV.

> DICK

Holy Mary, Mother of God.

> ALABAMA

This is great, we got cable.

> CLARENCE
> (*to Alabama*)

Bama, you got your blade?

Keeping her eyes on the TV, she pulls out from her purse a Swiss army knife with a tiny dinosaur on it and tosses it to Clarence. Clarence takes off the corkscrew and opens the wine.

He pours some wine into a couple of hotel plastic cups, a big glass for Dick, a little one for himself. He hands it to Dick. Dick takes it and drinks.

> DICK

This shit can't be real.

> CLARENCE

It'll get ya high.

He tosses Dick the knife.

Do you want some wine, sweetheart?

> ALABAMA

Nope. I'm not really a wine gal.

Using the knife, Dick snorts some of the cocaine. He jumps back.

> DICK

It's fuckin' real!

> (*to Clarence*)

It's fuckin' real!

186

CLARENCE

I certainly hope so.

DICK

You've got a helluva lotta coke there, man!

CLARENCE

I know.

DICK

Do you have any idea how much fuckin' coke you got?

CLARENCE

Tell me.

DICK

I don't know! A fuckin' lot!

He downs his wine. Clarence fills his glass.

This is Drexl's coke!?

CLARENCE

Drexl's dead. This is Clarence's coke and Clarence can do whatever he wants with it. And what Clarence wants to do is sell it. Then me and Bama are gonna leave on a jet plane and spend the rest of our lives spendin'. So, you got my letter, have you lined up any buyers?

DICK

Look, Clarence, I'm not Joe Cocaine.

Dick gulps half of his wine. Clarence fills it up.

CLARENCE

But you're an actor. I hear these Hollywood guys have it delivered to the set.

DICK

Yeah, they do. And maybe when I start being a successful actor I'll know those guys. But most of the people I know are like me. They ain't got a pot to piss in or a window to throw it out of. Now, if you want to sell a little bit at a time –

CLARENCE

No way! The whole enchilada in one shot.

DICK

Do you have any idea how difficult that's gonna be?

CLARENCE

I'm offering a half a million dollars' worth of white for two hundred thousand. How difficult can that be?

DICK

It's difficult because you're sellin' it to a particular group. Big shots. Fat cats. Guys who can use that kind of quantity. Guys who can afford two hundred thousand. Basically, guys I don't know. You don't know. And, more important, they don't know you. I did talk with one guy who could possibly help you.

CLARENCE

Is he big league?

DICK

He's nothing. He's in my acting class. But he works as an assistant to a very powerful movie producer named Lee Donowitz. I thought Donowitz could be interested in a deal like this. He could use it. He could afford it.

CLARENCE

What'd'ya tell 'em?

DICK

Hardly anything. I wasn't sure from your letter what was bullshit, and what wasn't.

CLARENCE

What's this acting class guy's name?

DICK

Elliot.

CLARENCE

Elliot what?

DICK

Elliot Blitzer.

CLARENCE

OK, call 'im up and arrange a meeting, so we can get through all the getting to know you stuff.

DICK

Where?

CLARENCE
(to Alabama)

Where?

ALABAMA

The zoo.

CLARENCE
(to Dick)

The zoo.
(pause)

What are you waiting for?

DICK

Would you just shut up a minute and let me think?

CLARENCE

What's to think about?

DICK

Shut up! First you come waltzing into my life after two years. You're married. You killed a guy.

CLARENCE

Two guys.

DICK

Two guys. Now you want me to help you with some big drug deal. Fuck, Clarence, you killed somebody and you're blowin' it off like it don't mean shit.

CLARENCE

Don't expect me to be all broken up over poor Drexl. I think he was a fuckin', freeloadin', parasitic scumbag, and he got exactly what he deserved. I got no pity for a mad dog like that. I think I should get a merit badge or somethin'.

189

Dick rests his head in his hands.

Look, buddy, I realize I'm layin' some pretty heavy shit on ya, but
I need you to rise to the occasion. So, drink some more wine. Get
used to the idea, and get your friend on the phone.

EXT. LOS ANGELES ZOO – DAY

CU – A black panther, the four-legged kind, paces back and forth.

*Clarence, Alabama, Dick, and Elliot Blitzer are walking through the
zoo. One look at Elliot and you can see what type of actor he is, a real
GQ, blow-dry boy. As they walk and talk, Clarence is eating a box of
animal crackers and Alabama is blowing soap bubbles.*

ELLIOT

So you guys got five hundred thousand dollars' worth of cola that
you're unloading –

CLARENCE

Want an animal cracker?

ELLIOT

Yeah, OK.

He takes one.

CLARENCE

Leave the gorillas.

ELLIOT

– that you're unloading for two hundred thousand dollars –

CLARENCE

Unloading? That's a helluva way to describe the bargain of a
lifetime.

DICK
(*trying to chill him out*)

Clarence . . .

ELLIOT

Where did you get it?

190

CLARENCE

I grow it on my window-sill. The light's really great there and I'm up high enough so you can't see it from the street.

ELLIOT
(*forcing a laugh*)

Ha ha ha. No really, where does it come from?

CLARENCE

Coco leaves. You see, they take the leaves and mash it down until it's kind of a paste –

ELLIOT
(*turning to Dick*)

Look, Dick, I don't –

CLARENCE
(*laughing*)

No problem, Elliot. I'm just fuckin' wit ya, that's all. Actually, I'll tell you but you gotta keep it quiet. Understand, if Dick didn't assure me you're good people I'd just tell ya, none of your fuckin' business. But, as a sign of good faith, here it goes: I gotta friend in the department.

ELLIOT

What department?

CLARENCE

What do you think, eightball?

ELLIOT

The police department?

CLARENCE

Duh. What else would I be talking about? Now stop askin' stupid doorknob questions. Well, a year and a half ago, this friend of mine got access to the evidence room for an hour. He snagged this coke. But, he's a good cop with a wife and a kid, so he sat on it for a year and a half until he found a guy he could trust.

ELLIOT

He trusts you?

CLARENCE

We were in Four H together. We've known each other since childhood. So, I'm handling the sales part. He's my silent partner, and he knows if I get fucked up, I won't drop dime on him. He's kinda paranoid. Now, no farther, you understand. I didn't tell you nothin' and you didn't hear nothin'.

ELLIOT

Sure. I didn't hear anything.

Elliot is more than satisfied. Clarence makes a comical face at Dick when Elliot's not looking. Dick is wearing an I-don't-believe-this-guy expression. Alabama is forever blowing bubbles.

CUT TO:

EXT. LOS ANGELES ZOO – SNACK BAR – DAY

We're in the snack bar area of the zoo. Alabama, Dick, and Elliot are sitting around a plastic outdoor table. Clarence is pacing around the table as he talks. Alabama is still blowing bubbles.

CLARENCE
(*to Elliot*)

Do I look like a beautiful blond with big tits and an ass that tastes like French vanilla ice-cream?

Elliot hasn't the slightest idea what that is supposed to mean.

ELLIOT

What?

CLARENCE

Do I look like a beautiful blond with big tits and an ass that tastes like French vanilla ice-cream?

ELLIOT
(*with conviction*)

No. No, you don't.

CLARENCE

Then why are you telling me all this bullshit just so you can fuck me?

192

DICK
(*trying to chill him out*)

Clarence . . .

CLARENCE
(*to Dick*)

Let me handle this.

ELLIOT

Get it straight, Lee isn't into taking risks. He deals with a couple of guys, and he's been dealing with them for years. They're reliable. They're dependable. And, they're safe.

CLARENCE

Riddle me this, Batman. If you're all so much in love with each other, what the fuck are you doing here? I'm sure you got better things to do with your time than walk around in circles starin' up a panther's ass. Your guy's interested because with that much shit at his fingertips he can play Joe fuckin' Hollywood till the wheels come off. He can sell it, he can snort it, he can play Santa Claus with it. At the price he's payin', he'll have the freedom to be able to just throw it around. He'll be everybody's best friend. And, you know, that's what we're talkin' about here. I'm not puttin' him down. Hey, let him run wild. Have a ball, it's his money. But, don't expect me to hang around forever waitin' for you guys to grow some guts.

Elliot has been silenced. He nods his head in agreement.

INT. PORSCHE – MOVING – MULHOLLAND DRIVE – DAY

Movie producer, Lee Donowitz, is driving his Porsche through the winding Hollywood hills, just enjoying being rich and powerful. His cellular car phone rings, he answers.

LEE

Hello.
(*pause*)

Elliot, it's Sunday. Why am I talkin' to you on Sunday? I don't see enough of you during the week I gotta talk to you on Sunday? Why is it you always call me when I'm on the windiest street in LA?

BACK TO: ELLIOT

Elliot is on the zoo payphone. Clarence is next to him. Dick is next to Clarence. Alabama is next to Dick, blowing bubbles.

> ELLIOT
> (*on phone*)
> I'm with that party you wanted me to get together with. Do you know what I'm talking about, Lee?

BACK TO: LEE

Store-fronts whiz by in the background.

> LEE
> Why the hell are you calling my phone to talk about that?

BACK TO: ELLIOT

> ELLIOT
> Well, he's here right now, and he insists on talking to you.

BACK TO: LEE

In the 7th Street tunnel. Lee's voice echoes.

> LEE
> Are you outta your fuckin' mind?

BACK TO: ELLIOT

> ELLIOT
> You said if I didn't get you on the –

Clarence takes the receiver out of Elliot's hand.

> CLARENCE
> (*into phone*)
> Hello, Lee, it's Clarence. At last we meet.

EXT. DICK'S APARTMENT – DAY

Virgil's knocking on Dick's door. Floyd (Dick's room-mate) answers.

> VIRGIL
> Hello, is Dick Ritchie here?

194

FLOYD

Naw, he ain't home right now.

VIRGIL

Do you live here?

FLOYD

Yeah, I live here.

VIRGIL

Sorta room-mates?

FLOYD

Exactly room-mates.

VIRGIL

Maybe you can help me. Actually, who I'm looking for is a friend
of ours from Detroit. Clarence Worley? I heard he was in town.
Might be traveling with a pretty girl named Alabama. Have you
seen him? Are they stayin' here?

FLOYD

Naw, they ain't stayin' here. But, I know who you're talkin'
about. They're stayin' at the Hollywood Holiday Inn.

VIRGIL

How do you know? You been there?

FLOYD

No, I ain't been there. But I heard him say it. Hollywood Holiday
Inn. Kinda easy to remember.

VIRGIL

You're right. It is.

EXT. LOS ANGELES ZOO — PAYPHONE — DAY

Clarence is still on the phone with Lee.

CLARENCE

Lee, the reason I'm talkin' with you is I want to open *Doctor
Zhivago* in LA. And I want you to distribute it.

BACK TO: LEE

195

Stopped in traffic on Sunset Boulevard.

                              LEE
I don't know, Clarence, *Doctor Zhivago*'s a pretty big movie.

BACK TO: CLARENCE

                           CLARENCE
The biggest. The biggest movie you've ever dealt with, Lee. We're talkin' a lot of film. A man'd have ta be an idiot not to be a little cautious about a movie like that. And Lee, you're no idiot.

BACK TO: LEE

He's still stuck on Sunset Boulevard, the traffic's moving better now.

                              LEE
I'm not sayin' I'm not interested. But being a distributor's not what I'm all about. I'm a film producer, I'm on this world to make good movies. Nothing more. Now, having my big toe dipped into the distribution end helps me on many levels.

Traffic breaks and Lee speeds along. The background whizzes past him.

But the bottom line is: I'm not Paramount. I have a select group of distributors I deal with. I buy their little movies. Accomplish what I wanna accomplish, end of story. Easy, business-like, very little risk.

BACK TO: CLARENCE

                           CLARENCE
Now that's bullshit, Lee. Every time you buy one of those little movies it's a risk. I'm not sellin' you something that's gonna play two weeks, six weeks, then go straight to cable. This is *Doctor Zhivago*. This'll be packin' 'em in for a year and a half. Two years! That's two years you don't have to work with anybody's movie but mine.

BACK TO: LEE

Speeding down a beachside road.

                              LEE
Well then, what's the hurry? Is it true the rights to *Doctor Zhivago* are in arbitration?

CLARENCE

I wanna be able to announce this deal at Cannes. If I had time for a courtship, Lee, I would. I'd take ya out, I'd hold your hand, I'd kiss you on the cheek at the door. But, I'm not in that position. I need to know if we're in bed together, or not. If you want my movie, Lee, you're just gonna have to come to terms with your Fear and Desire.

Pause. Clarence hands the phone to Elliot.

(*to Elliot*)

He wants ta talk to ya.

ELLIOT
(*into phone*)

Mr Donowitz?

(*pause*)

I told you, through Dick.

(*pause*)

He's in my acting class.

(*pause*)

About a year.

(*pause*)

Yeah, he's good.

(*pause*)

They grew up together.

(*pause*)

Sure thing.

Elliot hangs up the phone.

He says Wednesday at three o'clock at the Beverly Wilshire. He wants everybody there.

(*pointing at Clarence*)

He'll talk to you. If after talkin' to you he's convinced you're OK, he'll do business. If not, he'll say fuck it and walk out the door. He also wants a sample bag.

CLARENCE

No problem on both counts.

197

He offers Elliot the animal crackers.

Have a cookie.

Elliot takes one.

                  ELLIOT

Thanks.

He puts in in his mouth.

                  CLARENCE

That wasn't a gorilla, was it?

EXT. HOLIDAY INN – DAY

The red Mustang with Clarence and Alabama pulls up to the hotel. Alabama hops out. Clarence stays in.

                  ALABAMA

You did it, Quickdraw, I'm so proud of you. You were like a ninja. Did I do my part OK?

                  CLARENCE

Babalouey, you were perfect, I could hardly keep from busting up.

                  ALABAMA

I felt so stupid just blowing those bubbles.

                  CLARENCE

You were chillin', kind of creepy even. You totally fucked with his head. I'm gonna go grab dinner.

                  ALABAMA

I'm gonna hop in the tub and get all wet, and slippery, and soapy. Then I'm gonna lie in the waterbed, not even both to dry off, and watch X-rated movies till you get your ass back to my lovin' arms.

They kiss.

                  CLARENCE

We now return you to *Bullit* already in progress.

He slams the Mustang in reverse and peels out of the hotel. Alabama walks her little walk from the parking lot to the pool area. Somebody whistles at her, she turns to them.

ALABAMA

Thank you.

She gets to her door, takes out the key, and opens her door.

INT. HOLLYWOOD HOLIDAY INN – CLARENCE'S ROOM – DAY

She steps in only to find Virgil sitting in a chair placed in front of the door with a sawed-off shutgun aimed right at her.

VIRGIL
(calmly)

Step inside and shut the door.

She doesn't move, she's frozen. Virgil leans forward.

(calmly)

Lady. I'm gonna shoot you in the face.

She does exactly as he says. Virgil rises, still aiming the sawed-off.

Step away from the door, move into the room.

She does. He puts the shotgun down on the chair, then steps closer to her.

OK, Alabama, where's our coke, where's Clarence, and when's he coming back.

ALABAMA

I think you got the wrong room, my name is Sadie. I don't have any Coke, but there's a Pepsi machine downstairs. I don't know any Clarence, but maybe my husband does. You might have heard of him, he plays football, Al Lylezado. He'll be home any minute, you can ask him.

Virgil can't help but smile.

VIRGIL

You're cute.

Virgil jumps up and does a mid-air kung fu kick which catches Alabama square in the face, lifting her off the ground and dropping her flat on her back.

INT. MOVING RED MUSTANG – DAY

Clarence, in his car, driving to get something to eat, singing to himself.

> CLARENCE
> (*singing*)
> 'Land of stardust, land of glamour,
> Vistavision and Cinerama,
> Everything about it is a must,
> To get to Hollywood, or bust . . .'

INT. HOLLYWOOD HOLIDAY INN – CLARENCE'S ROOM – DAY

Alabama's laying flat. She actually blacks out for a moment, but the salty taste of the blood in her mouth wakes her up. She opens her eyes and sees Virgil standing there, smiling. She closes them, hoping it's a dream. They open again to the same sight. She has never felt more helpless in her life.

> VIRGIL
> Hurts, don't it? It better. Took me a long time to kick like that. I'm a third-degree blackbelt, you know? At home I got trophies. Tournaments I was in. Kicked all kinds of ass. I got great technique. You ain't hurt that bad. Get on your feet, Fruitloop.

Alabama wobbily complies.

> Where's our coke? Where's Clarence? And when's he comin' back?

Alabama looks in Virgil's eyes and realizes that without a doubt she's going to die, because this man is going to kill her.

> ALABAMA
> Go take a flying fuck at a rolling donut.

Virgil doesn't waste a second. He gives her a side kick straight to the stomach. The air is sucked out of her lungs. She falls to her knees. She's on all fours gasping for air that's just not there.

Virgil whips out a pack of Lucky Strikes. He lights one up with a Zippo lighter. He takes a long, deep drag.

200

VIRGIL
Whatsamatta? Can't breathe? Get used to it.

INT. HAMBURGER STAND – DAY

Clarence walks through the door of some mom and pop fast-food restaurant.

CLARENCE
Woah! Smells like hamburgers in here! What's the biggest, fattest hamburger you guys got?

The Iranian Guy at the counter says:

IRANIAN GUY
That would be Steve's double chili cheeseburger.

CLARENCE
Well, I want two of them bad boys. Two large orders of chili fries. Two large Diet Cokes.
    (*looking at menu on wall*)
And I'll tell you what, why don't you give me a combination burrito as well.

INT. HOLLYWOOD HOLIDAY INN – CLARENCE'S ROOM – DAY

Alabama is violently thrown into a corner of the room. She braces herself against the walls. She is very punchy. Virgil steps in front of her.

VIRGIL
You think your boyfriend would go through this kind of shit for you? Dream on, cunt. You're nothin' but a fuckin' fool. And your pretty face is gonna turn awful goddamn ugly in about two seconds. Now where's my fuckin' coke?

She doesn't answer. He delivers a spinning roundhouse kick to the head. Her head slams into the left side of the wall.

Where's Clarence?!

Nothing. He gives her another kick to the head, this time from the other side. Her legs start to give way. He catches her and throws her back. He slaps her lightly in the face to revive her, she looks at him.

201

When's Clarence getting back?

She can barely raise her arm, but she somehow manages, and she gives him the middle finger. Virgil can't help but smile.

You gotta lot of heart, kid.

He gives her a spinning roundhouse kick to the head that sends her to the floor.

INT. HAMBURGER STAND – DAY

CU – Burgers sizzling on a griddle. Chili and cheese is put on them.

Clarence is waiting for his order. He notices a Customer reading a copy of Newsweek *with Elvis on the cover.*

CLARENCE

That's a great issue.

The Customer lowers his magazine a little bit.

CUSTOMER

Yeah, I subscribe. It's a pretty decent one.

CLARENCE

Have you read the story on Elvis.

CUSTOMER

No. Not yet.

CLARENCE

You know, I saw it on the stands, my first inclination was to buy it. But, I look at the price and say forget it, it's just gonna be the same old shit. I ended up breaking down and buying it a few days later. Man, was I ever wrong.

CUSTOMER

Liked it, huh?

CLARENCE

It's probably the single best piece I've ever read about Elvis in my life.

CUSTOMER

That good, huh?

He takes the magazine from the Customer's hands and starts flipping to the Elvis article.

CLARENCE

It tried to pin down what the attraction is after all these years. It covers the whole spectrum of fans, the people who love his music, the people who grew up with him, the artists he inspired – Bob Dylan, Bruce Springsteen, and the fanatics, like these guys. I don't know about you, but they give me the creeps.

CUSTOMER

I can see what you mean.

CLARENCE

Like, look at her. She looks like she fell off of an ugly tree and hit every branch on the way down. Elvis wouldn't fuck her with Pat Boone's dick.

Clarence and the Customer laugh.

INT. HOLLYWOOD HOLIDAY INN – CLARENCE'S ROOM – DAY

Alabama's pretty beat up. She has a fat lip and her face is black and blue. She's crawling around on the floor. Virgil is tearing the place apart looking for the cocaine. He's also carrying on a running commentary.

VIRGIL

Now the first guy you kill is always the hardest. I don't care if you're the Boston Strangler or Wyatt Earp. You can bet that Texas boy, Charles Whitman, the fella who shot all them guys from that tower, I'll bet you green money that that first little black dot that he took a bead on, was the bitch of the bunch. No foolin', the first one's a tough row to hoe. Now, the second one, while it ain't no Mardi Gras, it ain't half as tough as the first. You still feel somethin' but it's just so diluted this time around. Then you completely level off on the third one. The third one's easy. It's gotten to the point now I'll do it just to watch their expression change.

He's tearing the motel room up in general. Then he flips the mattress up off the bed, and the black suitcase is right there.

Alabama is crawling, unnoticed, to where her purse is lying.

Virgil flips open the black case and almost goes snowblind.

> Well, well, well, looky here. I guess I just reached journey's end. Great. One less thing I gotta worry about.

Virgil closes the case. Alabama sifts through her purse.

She pulls out her Swiss army knife, opens it up. Virgil turns toward her.

VIRGIL
> OK, Sugarpop, we've come to what I like to call the moment of truth –

Alabama slowly rises clutching the thrust-out knife in both hands. Mr Karate-man smiles.

> Kid, you gotta lot a heart.

He moves toward her.

Alabama's hands are shaking.

> Tell you what I'm gonna do. I'm gonna give you a free swing. Now, I only do that for people I like.

He moves close.

Alabama's eyes study him. He grabs the front of his shirt and rips it open. Buttons fly everywhere.

> Go ahead, girl, take a stab at it.
> (*giggling*)
> You don't have anything to lose.

CU – Alabama's face. Virgil's right, she doesn't have anything to lose. Virgil's also right about this being the moment of truth. The ferocity in women that comes out at certain times, and is just there under the surface in many women all of the time, is unleashed. The absolute feeling of helplessness she felt only a moment ago has taken a one hundred and eighty degree turn into 'I'll take this motherfucker with me if it's the last thing I do' seething hatred.

Letting out a bloodcurdling yell, she raises the knife high above her head, then drops to her knees and plunges it deep into Virgil's right foot.

CU – Virgil's face. Talk about bloodcurdling yells.

Alabama is kicked in the teeth with Virgil's left foot.

Virgil bends down and carefully pulls the knife from his foot, tears running down his face.

While Virgil's bent down, Alabama smashes an Elvis Presley whiskey decanter Clarence bought her in Oklahoma over his head. It's only made of plaster, so it doesn't kill him.

Virgil's moving toward Alabama, limping on his bad foot.

> VIRGIL
>
> OK, no more Mr Nice-guy.

Alabama picks up the hotel TV and tosses it to him. He instinctively catches it and, with his arms full of television, Alabama cold-cocks him with her fist in his nose, breaking it.

Her eyes go straight to the door, then to the sawed-off shotgun by it. She runs to it, bends over the chair for the gun. Virgil's left foot kicks her in the back, sending her flying over the chair and smashing into the door.

Virgil furiously throws the chair out of the way and stands over Alabama. Alabama's lying on the ground laughing. Virgil has killed a lot of people, but not one of them has ever laughed before he did it.

> VIRGIL
>
> What's so funny?!!

> ALABAMA
> *(laughing)*
>
> You look so ridiculous.

She laughs louder. Virgil's insane. He picks her off the floor, then lifts her off the ground and throws her through the glass shower door in the bathroom.

> VIRGIL
>
> Laugh it up, cunt. You were in hysterics a minute ago. Why ain't you laughing now?

205

Alabama, lying in the bathtub, grabs a small bottle of hotel shampoo and squeezes it out in her hand.

Virgil reaches in the shower and grabs hold of her hair.

Alabama rubs the shampoo in his face. He lets go of her and his hands go to his eyes.

Oh Jesus!

She grabs hold of a hefty piece of broken glass and plunges it into his face.

Oh Mary, help me!

The battered and bruised and bloody Alabama emerges from the shower. She's clutching a big, bloody piece of broken glass. She's vaguely reminiscent of a Tasmanian devil. Poor Virgil can't see very well, but he sees her figure coming toward him. He lets out a wild haymaker that catches her in the jaw and knocks her into the toilet.

She recovers almost immediately and takes the porcelain lid off the back of the toilet tank.

Virgil whips out a .45 automatic from his shoulder holster, just as Alabama brings the lid down on his head. He's pressed up against the wall with this toilet lid hitting him. He can't get a good shot in this tight environment, but he fires anyway, hitting the floor, the wall, the toilet, and the sink.

The toilet lid finally shatters against Virgil's head. He falls to the ground.

Alabama goes to the medicine cabinet and whips out a big can of Final Net hairspray. She pulls a Bic lighter out of her pocket, and, just as Virgil raises his gun at her, she flicks the Bic and sends a stream of hairspray through the flame, which results in a big ball of fire that hits Virgil right in the face.

He fires off two shots. One hits the wall, another hits the sink pipe, sending water spraying.

Upon getting his face fried Virgil screams and jumps up, knocking Alabama down, and runs out of the bathroom.

Virgil collapses on to the floor of the living room. Then, he sees the sawed-off laying on the ground. He crawls toward it.

Alabama, in the bathroom, sees where he's heading. She picks up the .45 automatic and fires at him. It's empty. She's on her feet and into the room.

He reaches the shotgun, his hands grasp it.

Alabama spots and picks up the bloody Swiss army knife. She takes a knife-first running-dive at Virgil's back. She hits him.

He arches up, firing the sawed-off into the ceiling, dropping the gun, and sending a cloud of plaster and stucco all over the room.

Alabama snatches the shotgun.

Arched over on his back Virgil and Alabama make eye contact.

The first blast hits him in the shoulder, almost tearing his arm off. The second hits him in the knee. The third plays hell with his chest.

Alabama then runs at him, hitting him in the head with the butt of the shotgun.

Ever since she's been firing it's as if some other part of her brain has been functioning independently. She's been absent-mindedly saying the prayer of Saint Francis of Assisi.

ALABAMA
Lord, make me an instrument of Thy peace;
where there is hatred, let me sow love;
where there is injury, pardon;
where there is doubt, faith;
where there is despair, hope;
where there is darkness, light;
and where there is sadness, joy.
    O Divine Master, grant that I may not
so much seek to be consoled as to console;
to be understod as to understand;
to be loved, as to love;
for it is in giving that we receive,
it is in pardoning that we are pardoned,
and it is in dying that we are born
to eternal life.

Clarence, who's been hearing gunshots, bursts through the door, gun drawn, only to see Alabama, hitting a dead guy on the head, with a shotgun.

CLARENCE

Honey?

She continues. He puts his gun away.

Sweetheart? Cops are gonna be here any minute.

She continues. He takes the gun away from her, and she falls to the ground. She lies on the floor trembling, continuing with the downward swings of her arms.

Clarence grabs the shotgun and the cocaine, and tosses Alabama over his shoulder.

CUT TO:

EXT. HOLLYWOOD HOLIDAY INN – DAY

Everybody is outside their rooms watching as Clarence walks through the pool area with his bundle. Sirens can be heard.

EXT. MOVING RED MUSTANG – DAY

Clarence is driving like mad. Alabama's passed out in the passenger seat. She's muttering to herself. Clarence has one hand on the steering wheel and the other strokes Alabama's hair.

CLARENCE

Sleep baby. Don't dream. Don't worry. Just sleep. You deserve better than this. I'm so sorry. Sleep my angel. Sleep peacefully.

EXT. MOTEL 6 – NIGHT

A new motel. Clarence's red Mustang is parked outside.

INT. MOTEL 6 – CLARENCE'S ROOM– NIGHT

Alabama, with a fat lip and a black and blue face, is asleep in bed.

INT. NOWHERE

Clarence is in a nondescript room speaking directly to camera. He's in a headshot.

CLARENCE

I feel so horrible about what she went through. That fucker really beat the shit out of her. She never told him where I was. It's like I always felt that the way she felt about me was a mistake. She couldn't really care that much. I always felt in the back of my mind, I don't know, she was jokin'. But, to go through that and remain loyal, it's very easy to be enraptured with words, but to remain loyal when it's easier, even excusable, not to – that's a test of oneself. That's true romance. I swear to God, I'll cut off my hands and gouge out my eyes before I'll ever let anything happen to that lady again.

CUT TO:

EXT. HOLLYWOOD HILLS – NIGHT

A wonderful, gracefully flowing shot of the Hollywood hills. Off in the distance we hear the roar of a car engine.

EXT. MULHOLLAND DRIVE – NIGHT

Vaaaarrrooooooommmm!!! A silver Porsche is driving hells bells, taking quick corners, pushing it to the edge.

INT. MOVING SILVER PORSCHE – NIGHT

Elliot Blitzer is the driver, standing on it. A blond, glitzy Coke Whore is sitting next to him. They're having a ball. Then they see a red and blue light flashing in the rear-view mirror. It's the cops.

ELLIOT

Fuck! I knew it! I knew it! I fucking knew it! I should have my head examined, driving like this!
                    (*he pulls over*)
Kandi, you gotta help me.

KANDI

What can I do?

209

He pulls out the sample bag of cocaine that Clarence gave him earlier.

ELLIOT

You gotta hold this for me.

KANDI

You must be high. Uh-uh. No way.

ELLIOT
(*frantically*)

Just put it in your purse!

KANDI

I'm not gonna put that shit in my purse.

ELLIOT

They won't search you, I promise. You haven't done anything.

KANDI

No way, José.

ELLIOT

Please, they'll be here any minute. Just put it in your bra.

KANDI

I'm not wearing a bra.

ELLIOT
(*pleading*)

Put it in your pants.

KANDI

No.

ELLIOT

You're the one who wanted to drive fast.

KANDI

Read my lips.

She mouths the word 'no'.

ELLIOT

After all I've done for you, you fucking whore!!

She goes to slap him, she hits the bag of cocaine instead. It rips open. Cocaine completely covers his blue suit. At that moment Elliot turns to face a flashlight beam. Tears fill his eyes.

Elliot is sitting in a chair at a table. Two young, good-looking, casually dressed, Starsky and Hutch-type Police Detectives are questioning him. They're known in the department as Nicholson and Dimes. The dark-haired one is Cody Nicholson, and the blond is Nicky Dimes.

NICHOLSON
Look, sunshine, we found a sandwich bag of uncut cocaine –

DIMES
Not a tiny little vial –

NICHOLSON
But a fuckin' baggie.

DIMES
Now don't sit there and feed us some shit.

NICHOLSON
You got caught. It's all fun and fuckin' games till you get caught. But now we gottcha. OK, Mr Elliot actor, you've just made the big time –

DIMES
You're no longer an extra –

NICHOLSON
Or a bit player –

DIMES
Or a supporting actor –

NICHOLSON
You're a fuckin' star! And you're gonna be playin' your little one-man show nightly for the next two fuckin' years for a captive audience –

DIMES
But there is a bright side though. If you ever have to play a part of a guy who gets fucked in his ass on a daily basis by throat-slitting niggers, you'll have so much experience to draw on –

NICHOLSON
And just think, when you get out in a few years, you'll meet some

211

girl, get married, and you'll be so understanding to your wife's needs, because you'll know what it's like to be a woman –

DIMES

'Course you'll wanna fuck her in the ass. Pussy just won't feel right anymore –

NICHOLSON

That is, of course, if you don't catch Aids from all your anal intrusions.

Elliot starts crying. Nicholson and Dimes exchange looks and smiles. Mission accomplished.

INT. POLICE STATION – CAPTAIN KRINKLE'S OFFICE – DAY

Captain Bufford Krinkle is sitting behind his desk, where he spends about seventy-five percent of his days. He's your standard rough, gruff, no-nonsense, by-the-book-type police captain.

KRINKLE

Nicholson! Dimes! Get in here!

The two casually dressed, sneaker-wearing cops rush in, both shouting at once.

NICHOLSON	DIMES
Krinkle, this is it. We got it, man. And it's all ours. I mean talk about fallin' into somethin'. You shoulda seen it, it was beautiful. Dimes is hittin' him from the left about being fucked in the ass by niggers, I'm hittin' him from the right about not likin' pussy anymore, finally he just starts cryin', and then it was all over –	Krinkle, you're lookin' at the two future cops of the month. We have it, and when I say we, I don't mean me and him, I'm referring to the whole department. Haven't had a decent bust this whole month. Well, we mighta come in like a lamb, but we're goin' out like a lion –

KRINKLE

Both you idiots, shut up, I can't understand shit! Now, what's happened, what's going on, and what are you talking about?

212

Okee-dokee. It's like this, Krinkle; a patrol car stops this dork for
speeding, they walk up to the window and the guy's covered in
coke. So they bring his ass in and me an' Nicholson go to work on
him –

NICHOLSON

Nicholson and I.

DIMES

Nicholson and I go to work on him. Now we know something's
rotten in Denmark, 'cause this dickhead had a big bag, and it's
uncut too, so we're sweatin' him, tryin' to find out where he got it.
Scarin' the shit outta him –

NICHOLSON

Which wasn't too hard, the guy was a real squid.

DIMES

So we got this guy scared shitless and he starts talkin'. And,
Krinkle, you ain't gonna fuckin' believe it.

CUT TO:

INT. RESTAURANT – DAY

*Detroit. Very fancy restaurant. Four wise-guy Hoods, one older, the other
three, youngsters, are seated at a table with Mr Coccotti.*

COCCOTTI

– And so, tomorrow morning comes, and no Virgil. I check with
Nick Cardella, who Virgil was supposed to leave my narcotics
with, he never shows. Now, children, somebody is stickin' a
red-hot poker up my asshole and what I don't know is whose
hand's on the handle.

YOUNG WISE-GUY #1 (FRANKIE)

You think Virgil started gettin' big ideas?

COCCOTTI

It's possible. Anybody can be carried away with delusions of
grandeur. But after that incident in Ann Arbor, I trust Virgil.

YOUNG WISE-GUY #2 (DARIO)

What happened?

OLD WISE-GUY (LENNY)

Virgil got picked up in a warehouse shakedown. He got five years, he served three.

COCCOTTI

Anybody who clams up and does his time, I don't care how I feel about him personally, he's OK.

BACK TO: KRINKLE'S OFFICE

NICHOLSON

It seems a cop from some department, we don't know where, stole a half a million dollars of coke from the property cage and he's been sittin' on it for a year and a half. Now the cops got this weirdo –

DIMES

Suspect's words –

NICHOLSON

To front for him. So Elliot is workin' out a deal between them and his boss, a big movie producer named Lee Donowitz.

DIMES

He produced *Comin' Home in a Body Bag*.

KRINKLE

That Vietnam movie?

NICHOLSON

Uh-huh.

KRINKLE

That was a good fuckin' movie.

DIMES

Sure was.

KRINKLE

Do you believe him?

214

NICHOLSON
I believe he believes him.

DIMES
He's so spooked he'd turn over his momma, his daddy, his two-panny granny, and Anna and the King of Siam if he had anything on him.

NICHOLSON
This rabbit'll do anything not to do time, including wearing a wire.

KRINKLE
He'll wear a wire?

DIMES
We talked him into it.

KRINKLE
Dirty cops. We'll have to bring in internal affairs on this.

NICHOLSON
Look, we don't care if you bring in the state militia, the volunteer fire department, the LA Thunderbirds, the ghost of Steve McQueen, and twelve Roman gladiators, so long as we get credit for the bust.

DIMES
Cocaine. Dirty cops. Hollywood. This is Crocket and Tubbs all the way. And we found it, so we want the fucking collar.

BACK TO:

INT. RESTAURANT – DAY

YOUNG WISE-GUY #3 (MARVIN)
Maybe Virgil dropped it off at Cardella's. Cardella turns Virgil's switch to off, and Cardella decides to open up his own fruit stand.

LENNY
Excuse me, Mr Coccotti.
                    (to Marvin)
Do you know Nick Cardella?

215

MARVIN

No.

LENNY

Then where the hell do you get off talkin' that kind of talk – ?

MARVIN

I didn't mean –

LENNY

Shut your mouth. Nick Cardella was provin' what his word was worth before you were in your daddy's nutsack. What sun do you walk under you can throw a shadow on Nick Cardella? Nick Cardella's a stand-up guy.

COCCOTTI

Children, we're digressing. Another possibility is that rat-fuck whore and her wack-a-doo cowboy boyfriend out-aped Virgil. Knowing Virgil, I find that hard to believe. But they sent Drexl to hell, and Drexl was no faggot. So you see, children, I got a lot of questions and no answers. Find out who this wing-and-a-prayer artist is and take him off at the neck.

TITLE CARD:

'THE BIG DAY'

EXT. IMPERIAL HIGHWAY – SUNRISE

Clarence's red Mustang is parked on top of a hill just off of Imperial Highway. As luck would have it, somebody has abandoned a ratty old sofa on the side of the road. Clarence and Alabama sit on the sofa, sharing a Jumbo Java, and enjoying the sunrise and wonderful view of the LAX Airport runways, where planes are taking off and landing. A plane takes off, and they stop and watch.

CLARENCE

Ya know, I used to fuckin' hate airports.

ALABAMA

Really?

216

CLARENCE

With a vengeance, I hated them.

ALABAMA

How come?

CLARENCE

I used to live by one back in Dearborn. It's real frustratin' to be surrounded by airplanes when you ain't got shit. I hated where I was, but I couldn't do anythin' about it. I didn't have any money. It was tough enough just tryin' to pay my rent every month, an' here I was livin' next to an airport. Whenever I went outside, I saw fuckin' planes takin' off. I'm tryin' to watch TV, fuckin' planes takin' off drownin' out my show. All day long I'm seein', hearin' people doin' what I wanted to do most, but couldn't.

ALABAMA

What?

CLARENCE

Leavin' Detroit. Goin' off on vacations, startin' new lives, business trips. Fun, fun, fun, fun.

Another plane takes off.

But knowin' me and you gonna be nigger-rich gives me a whole new outlook. I love airports now. Me 'n' you can get on any one of those planes out there, and go anywhere we want.

ALABAMA

You ain't kiddin', we got lives to start over, we should go somewhere where we can really start from scratch.

CLARENCE

I been in America all my life. I'm due for a change. I wanna see what TV in other countries is like. Besides, it's more dramatic. Where should we fly off to, my little turtledove?

ALABAMA

Cancoon.

CLARENCE

Why Cancoon?

217

ALABAMA

It's got a nice ring to it. It sounds like a movie. *Clarence and Alabama Go to Cancoon*. Don'cha think?

CLARENCE

But in my movie, baby, you get top billing.

They kiss.

Don't you worry 'bout anythin. It's all gonna work out for us. We deserve it.

INT. DICK'S APARTMENT – DAY

Dick, Clarence and Alabama are just getting ready to leave for the drug deal. Floyd lays on the couch watching TV. Alabama's wearing dark glasses because of the black eye she has.

CLARENCE
(*to Floyd*)

You sure that's how you get to the Beverly Wilshire?

FLOYD

I've partied there twice. Yeah, I'm sure.

DICK

Yeah, well if we get lost, it's your ass.
(*to Clarence*)

Come on, Clarence, let's go. Elliot's going to meet us in the lobby.

CLARENCE

I'm just makin' sure we got everything.
(*pointing to Alabama*)

You got yours?

She holds up the suitcase. The phone rings. The three pile out the door. Floyd picks up the phone.

FLOYD

Hello?

He puts his hand over the receiver.

Dick, it's for you. You here?

No. I left.

He starts to close the door then opens it again.

I'll take it.
> *(he takes the receiver)*

Hello.
> *(pause)*

Hi, Catherine, I was just walkin' out the –
> *(pause)*

Really?
> *(pause)*

I don't believe it.
> *(pause)*

She really said that?
> *(pause)*

I'll be by first thing.
> *(pause)*

No, thank you for sending me out.
> *(pause)*

Bye, bye.

He hangs up and looks at Clarence.

> *(stunned)*

I got the part on *T. J. Hooker*.

CLARENCE

No shit? Dick, that's great!

Clarence and Alabama are jumping around. Floyd even smiles.

DICK
> *(still stunned)*

They didn't even want a callback. They just hired me like that.
Me and Peter Breck are the two heavies. We start shooting
Monday. My call is for seven o'clock in the morning.

CLARENCE

Ah, Dick, let's talk about it in the car. We can't be late.

Dick looks at Clarence. He doesn't want to go.

                              DICK
    Clarence.

                            CLARENCE
    Yeah?

                              DICK
    Um, nothing. Let's go.

They exit.

EXT. LAX AIRPORT – HOTEL – DAY

We see the airport and move in closer on a hotel on the landscape.

INT. LAX AIRPORT – HOTEL ROOM – DAY

Lenny can be seen putting a shotgun together. He is sitting on a bed.

Dario enters the frame with his own shotgun. He goes over to Lenny and gives him some shells.

Marvin walks through the frame cocking his own shotgun.

The bathroom door opens behind Lenny and Frankie walks out twirling a couple of .45 automatics in his hands.

INT. BEVERLY WILSHIRE – COPS' HOTEL ROOM – DAY

Nicholson and Dimes and four Detectives from internal affairs are in a room on the same floor as Donowitz. They have just put a wire on Elliot.

                            NICHOLSON
    OK, say something.

                              ELLIOT
                    (*talking loud into the wire*)
    Hello! Hello! Hello! How now brown cow!

                              DIMES
    Just talk regular.

                               220

ELLIOT
(*normal tone*)
'But, soft! what light through yonder window breaks?
It is the east and Juliet is the sun.
Arise, fair sun, and kill the envious moon,
Who is already sick and pale with grief – '

NICHOLSON
Are you getting this shit?

DETECTIVE BY TAPE MACHINE
Clear as a bell.

Nicholson, Dimes, and the head IA Officer, Wurlitzer, huddle by Elliot.

DIMES
Now, remember, we'll be monitoring just down the hall.

ELLIOT
And if there's any sign of trouble you'll come in.

NICHOLSON
Like gang-busters. Now, remember, if you don't want to go to
jail, we gotta put your boss in jail.

DIMES
We have to show in court that, without a doubt, a successful man,
an important figure in the Hollywood community, is also dealing
cocaine.

NICHOLSON
So you gotta get him to admit on tape that he's buying this coke.

WURLITZER
And this fellow Clarence?

ELLIOT
Yeah, Clarence.

WURLITZER
You gotta get him to name the police officer behind all this.

ELLIOT
I'll try.

DIMES
You do more than try.

NICHOLSON
You do.

DIMES
Hope you're a good actor, Elliot.

INT. MOVING RED MUSTANG – DAY

Clarence, Dick, and Alabama en route.

DICK
You got that playing basketball?

ALABAMA
Yeah. I got elbowed right in the eye. And if that wasn't enough, I got hurled the ball when I'm not looking. Wham! Right in my face.

They stop at a red light. Clarence looks at Alabama.

CLARENCE
Red light means love, baby.

He and Alabama start kissing.

INT. MOVING CADILLAC – DAY

Marvin, Frankie, Lenny, and Dario in a rented Caddy.

INT. BEVERLY WILSHIRE PARKING LOT – DAY

Clarence, Alabama, and Dick get out of the Mustang. Dick takes the suitcase.

CLARENCE
I'll take that. Now, remember, both of you, let me do the talking.

Clarence takes out his .45. Dick reacts. They walk and talk.

DICK
What the fuck did you bring that for?

In case.

DICK

In case of what?

CLARENCE

In case they try to kill us. I don't know, what do you want me to say?

DICK

Look, Dillinger, Lee Donowitz is not a pimp –

CLARENCE

I know that, Richard. I don't think I'll need it. But something this last week has taught me, it's better to have a gun and not need it than to need a gun and not have it.

Pause. Clarence stops walking.

Hold it, guys. I don't know about the rest of you, but I'm pretty scared. What say we forget the whole thing.

Dick and Alabama are both surprised and relieved.

DICK

Do you really mean it?

CLARENCE

No, I don't really mean it. Well, I mean, this is our last chance to think about it. How 'bout you, Bama?

ALABAMA

I thought it was what you wanted, Clarence.

CLARENCE

It is what I want. But I don't want to spend the next ten years in jail. I don't want you guys to go to jail. We don't know what could be waiting for us up there. It'll probably be just what it's supposed to be. The only thing that's waiting for us is two hundred thousand dollars. I'm just looking at the downside.

DICK

Now's a helluva time to play 'what if.'

223

CLARENCE

This is our last chance to play 'what if.' I want to do it. I'm just scared of getting caught.

ALABAMA

It's been fun thinking about the money but I can walk away from it, honey.

CLARENCE

That rhymes.

He kisses her.

DICK

Well, if we're not gonna do it, let's just get in the car and get the fuck outta here.

CLARENCE

Yeah, let's just get outta here.

The three walk back to the car. Clarence gets behind the wheel. The other two climb in. Clarence hops back out.

I'm sorry, guys, I gotta do it. As petrified as I am, I just can't walk away. I'm gonna be kicking myself in the ass for the rest of my life if I don't go in there. Lee Donowitz isn't a gangster lookin' to skin us, and he's not a cop, he's a famous movie producer lookin' to get high. And I'm just the man who can get him there. So what say we throw caution to the wind and let the chips fall where they may.

Clarence grabs the suitcase and makes a beeline for the hotel. Dick and Alabama exchange looks and follow.

INT. BEVERLY WILSHIRE – LOBBY – DAY

Elliot's walking around the lobby. He's very nervous, so he's singing to himself.

ELLIOT
(*singing*)

There's a man who leads a life of danger.
To everyone he meets

224

he stays a stranger.
Be careful what you say,
you'll give yourself away . . .

INT. BEVERLY WILSHIRE – COPS' HOTEL ROOM – DAY

Nicholson, Dimes, Wurlitzer, and the three other Detectives surround the tape machine. Coming from the machine:

ELLIOT'S VOICE
(off)

. . . odds are you won't live
to see tomorrow,
Secret agent man,
Secret agent man . . .

Nicholson looks at Dimes.

NICHOLSON

Why, all of sudden, have I got a bad feeling?

BACK TO: LOBBY

Clarence enters the lobby alone, he's carrying the suitcase. He spots Elliot and goes in his direction. Elliot sees Clarence approaching him. He says to himself, quietly:

ELLIOT

Elliot, your motivation is to stay out of jail.

Clarence walks up to Elliot, they shake hands.

Where's everybody else?

CLARENCE

They'll be along.

Alabama and Dick enter the lobby, they join up with Clarence and Elliot.

ELLIOT

Hi, Dick.

DICK

How you doin', Elliot?

225

CLARENCE

Well, I guess it's about that time.

ELLIOT

I guess so. Follow me.

INT. BEVERLY WILSHIRE – ELEVATOR – DAY

The four of them are riding up in the elevator. As luck would have it, they have the car to themselves. Rinky-dink elevator Muzak is playing. They are all silent. Clarence breaks the silence.

CLARENCE

Elliot.

ELLIOT

Yeah?

CLARENCE

Get on your knees.

Not sure he heard him right.

ELLIOT

What?

Clarence hits the stop button on the elevator panel and whips out his .45.

CLARENCE

I said, get on your fuckin' knees!

Elliot does it immediately. Dick and Alabama react.

Shut up, both of you, I know what I'm doin'!

BACK TO: COPS' HOTEL ROOM

Pandemonium.

DIMES

He knows.

NICHOLSON

How the fuck could he know?

DIMES
He saw the wire.

NICHOLSON
How's he supposed to see the wire?

DIMES
He knows something's up.

NICHOLSON
He's bluffing. He can't know.

BACK TO: ELEVATOR

Clarence puts the .45 against Elliot's forehead.

CLARENCE
You must think I'm pretty stupid, don't you?

No answer.

Don't you?

ELLIOT
(petrified)
No.

CLARENCE
(yelling)
Don't lie to me, motherfucker. You apparently think I'm the
dumbest motherfucker in the world! Don't you? Say: Clarence,
you are without a doubt, the dumbest motherfucker in the whole
wide world. Say it!

BACK TO: COPS

DIMES
We gotta get him outta there.

NICHOLSON
Whatta we gonna do? He's in an elevator.

BACK TO: ELEVATOR

CLARENCE
Say it, goddamn it!

ELLIOT

You are the dumbest person in the world.

CLARENCE

Apparently I'm not as dumb as you thought I am.

ELLIOT

No. No you're not.

CLARENCE

What's waiting for us up there. Tell me or I'll pump two right in your face.

BACK TO: COPS

NICHOLSON

He's bluffing ya, Elliot. Can't you see that? You're an actor, remember, the show must go on.

DIMES

This guy's gonna kill him.

BACK TO: ELEVATOR

CLARENCE

Stand up.

Elliot does. The .45 is still pressed against his forehead.

Like Nick Carter used to say: If I'm wrong, I'll apologize. I want you to tell me what's waitin' for us up there. Something's amiss. I can feel it. If anything out of the ordinary goes down, believe this, you're gonna be the first one shot. Trust me. I am AIDS, you fuck me, you die. Now quit making me mad and tell me why I'm so fucking nervous!

BACK TO: COPS

NICHOLSON

He's bluffin', I knew it. He doesn't know shit.

DIMES

Don't blow it, Elliot. He's bluffin'. He just told you so himself.

NICHOLSON

You're an actor, so act, motherfucker.

228

BACK TO: ELEVATOR

Elliot still hasn't answered.

CLARENCE

OK.

With the .45 up against Elliot's head Clarence puts his palm over the top of the gun to shield himself from the splatter. Alabama and Dick can't believe what he's gonna do.

Elliot, tears running down his face, starts talking for the benefit of the people at the other end of the wire. He sounds like a little boy.

ELLIOT

I don't wanna be here. I wanna go home. I wish somebody would just come and get me 'cause I don't like this. This is not what I thought it would be. And I wish somebody would just take me away. Just take me away. Come and get me. 'Cause I don't like this anymore. I can't take this. I'm sorry but I just can't. So, if somebody would just come to my rescue, everything would be all right.

BACK TO: COPS

Nicholson and Dimes shake their heads. They have a 'well, that's that' expression on their faces.

BACK TO: ELEVATOR

Clarence puts down the gun and hugs Elliot.

CLARENCE

Sorry, Elliot. Nothing personal. I just hadda make sure you're all right. I'm sure. I really apologize for scaring you so bad, but believe me, I'm just as scared as you. Friends?

Elliot, in a state of shock, takes Clarence's hand. Dick and Alabama are relieved.

BACK TO: COPS

Nicholson and Dimes listen open-mouthed, not believing what they're hearing.

INT. DICK'S APARTMENT – DAY

Floyd still lying on the couch watching TV. He hasn't moved since we last saw him.

There is a knock from the door.

                    FLOYD
            (*not turning away from TV*)
    It's open.

The front door flies open and the four Wise-guys rapidly enter the room. The door slams shut. All have their sawed-offs drawn and pointing at Floyd.

                    FLOYD
    Yes.

                    LENNY
    Are you Dick Ritchie?

                    FLOYD
    No.

                    LENNY
    Do you know a Clarence Worley?

                    FLOYD
    Yes.

                    LENNY
    Do you know where we can find him?

                    FLOYD
    He's at the Beverly Wilshire.

                    LENNY
    Where's that?

                    FLOYD
    Well, you go down Beechwood . . .

INT. BEVERLY WILSHIRE – LEE'S HOTEL ROOM– DAY

CU – A fist knocking on a door.

The door opens and reveals an extremely muscular guy with an Uzi strapped to his shoulder standing in the doorway, his name is Monty.

MONTY

Hi, Elliot. Are these your friends?

ELLIOT

You could say that. Everybody, this is Monty.

MONTY

C'mon in. Lee's in the can. He'll be out in a quick.

They all move into the room, it is very luxurious.

Another incredibly muscular guy, Boris, is sitting on the sofa, he too has an Uzi. Monty begins patting everybody down.

Sorry, nothing personal.

He starts to search Clarence. Clarence backs away.

CLARENCE

No need to search me, daredevil. All you'll find is a .45 calibre automatic.

Boris gets up from the couch.

BORIS

What compelled you to bring that along?

CLARENCE

The same thing that compelled you, Beastmaster, to bring rapid-fire weaponry to a business meeting.

BORIS

I'll take that.

CLARENCE

You'll have to.

The toilet flushes in the bathroom. The door swings open and Lee Donowitz emerges.

LEE

They're here. Who's who?

231

ELLIOT

Lee, this is my friend Dick, and these are his friends, Clarence and Alabama.

BORIS
(*pointing at Clarence*)

This guy's packin'.

LEE

Really?

CLARENCE

Well, I have to admit, walkin' through the door and seein' these *Soldier of Fortune* poster boys made me a bit nervous. But, Lee, I'm fairly confident that you came here to do business, not to be a wise-guy. So, if you want, I'll put the gun on the table.

LEE

I don't think that'll be necessary. Let's all have a seat. Boris, why don't you be nice and get coffee for everybody.

They all sit around a fancy glass table except for Boris, who's getting the coffee, and Monty, who's standing behind Lee's chair.

CLARENCE

Oh, Mr Donowitz –

LEE

Lee, Clarence. Please don't insult me. Call me Lee.

CLARENCE

OK, sorry, Lee. I just wanna tell you that *Comin' Home in a Body Bag* is one of my favourite movies. After *Apocalypse Now* I think it's the best Vietnam movie ever.

LEE

Thank you very much, Clarence.

CLARENCE

You know, most movies that win a lot of Oscars, I can't stand. *Sophie's Choice, Ordinary People, Kramer vs. Kramer, Gandhi.* All that stuff is safe, geriatric, coffee-table dog shit.

I hear you talkin', Clarence. We park our cars in the same
garage.

CLARENCE
Like that Merchant–Ivory clap-trap. All those assholes make are
unwatchable movies from unreadable books.

*Boris starts placing clear-glass coffee cups in front of everybody and fills
everybody's cup from a fancy coffee pot that he handles like an expert.*

LEE
Clarence, there might be somebody somewhere that agrees with
you more than I do, but I wouldn't count on it.

Clarence is on a roll and he knows it.

CLARENCE
They ain't plays, they ain't books, they certainly ain't movies,
they're films. And do you know what films are? They're for
people who don't like movies. *Mad Max*, that's a movie. *The
Good, the Bad, and the Ugly*, that's a movie. *Rio Bravo*, that's a
movie. *Rumble Fish*, that's a fuckin' movie. And, *Comin' Home
in a Body Bag*, that's a movie. It was the first movie with balls to
win a lot of Oscars since *The Deer Hunter*.

BACK TO: COPS

They're all listening to this.

DIMES
What's this guy doin'? Makin' a drug deal or gettin' a job on the
New Yorker?

BACK TO: LEE'S ROOM

CLARENCE
My uncle Roger and uncle Cliff, both of which were in Nam,
saw *Comin' Home in a Body Bag* and thought it was the most
accurate Vietnam film they'd ever seen.

LEE
You know, Clarence, when a veteran of that bullshit war says
that, it makes the whole project worthwhile. Clarence, my

friend, and I call you my friend because we have similar interests, let's take a look at what you have for me.

BACK TO: COPS

NICHOLSON

Thank God.

BACK TO: LEE

Clarence puts the suitcase on the table.

CLARENCE

Lee, when you see this you're gonna shit.

BACK TO: LOBBY

The four Wise-guys are at the desk.

LENNY
(*quietly to the others*)
What was the Jew-boy's name?

MARVIN

Donowitz, he said.

FRONT-DESK GUY

How can I help you, gentlemen?

LENNY

Yeah, we're from Warner Bros. What room is Mr Donowitz in?

BACK TO: LEE

Lee's looking over the cocaine and sampling it.

CLARENCE

Now that's practically uncut. You could, if you so desire, cut it a helluva lot more.

LEE

Don't worry, I'll desire. Boris, could I have some more coffee.

CLARENCE

Me too, Boris.

Boris fills both of their cups. They both, calm as a lake, take cream and sugar. All eyes are on them. Lee uses light cream and sugar, he begins stirring his cup. Clarence uses very heavy cream and sugar.

LEE
(*stirring loudly*)
You like a little coffee with your cream and sugar?

CLARENCE
I'm not satisfied till the spoon stands straight up.

Both are cool as cucumbers.

LEE
I have to hand it to you, this is not nose garbage, this is quality. Can Boris make anybody a sandwich? I got all kinds of sandwich shit from Canters in there.

ALABAMA
No thank you.

DICK
No. But thanks.

CLARENCE
No thanks, my stomach's a little upset. I ate somethin' at a restaurant that made me a little sick.

LEE
Where'd you go?

CLARENCE
A Norms in Van Nuys.

LEE
Bastards. That's why I always eat at Lawreys.

Lee continues looking at the merchandise.

Alabama writes something on her napkin with a pencil. She slides the napkin over to Clarence. It says: 'You're so cool' with a tiny heart drawn on the bottom of it. Clarence takes the pencil and draws an arrow through the heart. She takes the napkin and puts it in her pocket.

Lee looks up.

OK, Clarence, the merchandise is perfect. But, whenever I'm offered a deal that's too good to be true, it's because it's a lie. Convince me you're on the level.

BACK TO: COPS

NICHOLSON

If he don't bite, we ain't got shit except possession.

DIMES

Convince him.

BACK TO: LEE

CLARENCE

Well, Lee, it's like this. You're getting the bargain of a lifetime because I don't know what the fuck I'm doing. You're used to dealin' with professionals. I'm not a professional. I'm a rank amateur. I could take that, and I could cut it, and I could sell it a little bit at a time, and make a helluva lot more money. But, in order to do that, I'd have to become a drug dealer. I'm not a drug dealer. And I don't want to be a drug dealer. Deal with cut-throat junkies, killers, worry about getting busted all of the time. Just meeting you here today scares the shit outta me, and you're not a junkie, a killer or a cop, you're a fucking movie-maker. I like you, and I'm still scared. I'm a punk kid who picked up a rock in the street, only to find out it's the Hope Diamond. It's worth a million dollars, but I can't get a million dollars for it. But, you can. So, I'll sell it to you for a couple a hundred thousand. You go to make a million. It's all found money to me anyway. Me and my wife are minimum wage kids, two hundred thousand is the world.

LEE

Elliot tells me you're fronting for a dirty cop.

CLARENCE

Well, Elliot wasn't supposed to tell you anythin'.
(*to Elliot*)
Thanks a lot, bigmouth. I knew you were a squid the moment I laid eyes on you. In my book, buddy, you're a piece of shit.

> (*to Lee*)

He's not a dirty cop, he's a good cop. He just saw his chance and he took it.

LEE

Why does he trust you?

CLARENCE

We grew up together.

LEE

If you don't know shit, why does he think you can sell it?

CLARENCE

I bullshitted him.

Lee starts laughing.

LEE

That's wild. This fucking guy's a madman. I love it. Marty, go in the other room and get the money.

Clarence, Alabama and Dick exchange looks.

BACK TO: COPS

Nicholson and Dimes exchange looks.

DIMES/NICHOLSON

Bingo!

BACK TO: ELEVATOR

The four Wise-guys are coming up.

BACK TO: LEE

LEE
> (*pointing at Alabama*)

What's your part in this?

ALABAMA

I'm his wife.

LEE
> (*referring to Dick*)

How 'bout you?

                            DICK
I know Elliot.

                            LEE
And Elliot knows me. Tell me, Clarence, what department does
your friend work in?

Dick and Alabama panic.

                          CLARENCE
                    (*without missing a beat*)
Carson County Sheriffs.

BACK TO: COPS

The internal affairs officers high five.

BACK TO: LEE

Monty brings in a briefcase of money and puts it down on the table.

                            LEE
Wanna count your money?

                          CLARENCE
Actually, they can count it. I'd like to use the little boys' room.

BACK TO: COPS

They all stand.

                           DIMES
OK, boys. Let's go get 'em.

INT. BEVERLY WILSHIRE – LEE'S HOTEL ROOM – BATHROOM –
DAY

*Clarence steps inside the bathroom and shuts the door. As soon as it's shut
he starts doing the twist. He can't believe he's pulled it off. He goes to the
toilet and starts taking a piss. He turns and sees Elvis sitting on the sink.*

                           ELVIS
Clarence, I gotta hand it to ya. You were cooler than cool.

                          CLARENCE
I was dying. I thought for sure everyone could see it on my face.

                            238

All anybody saw was Clint Eastwood drinkin' coffee.

CLARENCE

Can you develop an ulcer in two minutes? Being cool is hard on your body.

ELVIS

Oh, and your line to Charles Atlas in there: 'I'll take that gun', 'You'll have to.'

CLARENCE

That was cool, wasn't it? You know, I don't even know where that came from. I just opened my mouth and it came out. After I said it I thought, that's a cool line, I gotta remember that.

BACK TO: LEE

Everything's just as it was.

Suddenly, Nicholson, Dimes, and the four Detectives break into the room with guns drawn.

NICHOLSON/DIMES

Police! Freeze, you're all under arrest!

Everybody at the table stands up. Boris and Monty stand ready with the Uzis.

NICHOLSON

You two! Put the guns on the floor and back away!

MONTY

Fuck you! All you pigs put your guns on the floor and back away.

LEE

Monty, what are you talking about? Do what they say.

DIMES

This is your last warning! Drop those fuckin' guns!

BORIS

This is your last warning! We could kill all six of ya and you fuckin' know it! Now get on the floor!

DICK
What the fuck am I doing here?

LEE
Boris! Everybody's gonna get killed! They're cops!

MONTY
So they're cops. Who gives a shit?

BORIS
Lee, something I never told you about me. I don't like cops.

DIMES
OK, let's everybody calm down and get nice. Nobody has to die.
We don't want it, and you don't want it.

LEE
We don't want it.

*The four Wise-guys burst through the door, shotguns drawn, except for
Frankie, who has two .45 automatics, one in each hand.*

Half of the cops spin around.

WURLITZER
Freeze!

LENNY
Who are you guys?

WURLITZER
Police.

DARIO
(*to Lenny*)
Do we get any extra if we have to kill cops?

BACK TO: BATHROOM

Clarence and Elvis.

CLARENCE
How do you think I'm doin' with Lee?

ELVIS
Are you kiddin'? He loves you.

CLARENCE

You don't think I'm kissin' his ass, do you?

ELVIS

You're tellin' him what he wants to hear, but that ain't the same thing as kissin' his ass.

CLARENCE

I'm not lyin' to him. I mean it. I loved *Comin' Home in a Body Bag.*

ELVIS

That's why it doesn't come across as ass-kissin', because it's genuine, and he can see that.

Elvis fixes Clarence's collar.

ELVIS

I like ya, Clarence. Always have.

BACK TO: LEE

This is a Mexican stand-off if ever there was one. Gangsters on one end with shotguns. Bodyguards with machine-guns on the other. And cops with handguns in the middle.

Dick's ready to pass out.

Alabama's so scared she pees on herself.

For Elliot, this has been the worst day of his life, and he's just about had it.

ELLIOT

Officer Dimes? Officer Dimes.

Dimes looks at Elliot.

This has nothing to do with me anymore. Can I just leave and you guys just settle it by yourselves?

DIMES

Elliot, shut the fuck up and stay put!

LEE
(*to Elliot*)

How did you know his name? How the fuck did he know your name? Why, you fuckin' little piece of shit!

241

ELLIOT
Lee, understand, I didn't want to –

NICHOLSON
Shut the fuck up!

LEE
Well, I hope you're not planning on acting any time in the next twenty years 'cause your career is over as of now! You might as well burn your SAG card! To think I treated you as a son! And you stabbed me in the heart!

Lee can't control his anger anymore. He grabs the coffee pot off the table and flings hot coffee into Elliot's face. Elliot screams and falls to his knees.

Instinctively, Nicholson shoots Lee twice.

Alabama screams.

Boris lets loose with his Uzi, painting Nicholson red with bullets.

DIMES
(*screaming*)
Cody!!!

Nicholson flies backwards.

Marvin fires his shotgun, hits Nicholson in the back, Nicholson's body jerks back and forth then on to the floor.

Clarence opens the bathroom door.

Dimes hits the ground firing.

A shot catches Clarence in the forehead.

Alabama screams.

Dario fires his sawed-off. It catches Clarence in the chest, hurling him on top of the bathroom sink, smashing the mirror.

It might have been a stand-off before, but once the firing starts everybody either hits the ground or runs for cover.

Dimes, Alabama, Dick, Lenny, an IA Officer and Wurlitzer hit the ground.

242

Boris dives into the kitchen area.

Monty tips the table over.

Marvin dives behind the sofa.

Dario runs out of the door and down the hall.

With bullets flying this way and that, some don't have time to do anything. Two IA Officers are shot right away.

Frankie takes an Uzi hit. He goes down firing both automatics.

Elliot gets it from both sides.

Alabama is crawling across the floor, like a soldier in war, towards the bathroom.

Clarence, still barely alive, lays on the sink, twitching. He moves and falls off.

Alabama continues crawling.

Marvin brings his sawed-off from behind the sofa and fires. The shotgun blast hits the glass table and Monty. Monty stands up screaming.

The Cops on the ground let loose, firing into Monty.

As Monty gets hit, his finger hits the trigger of the Uzi, spreading fire all over the apartment.

EXT. BEVERLY WILSHIRE – DAY

Cop cars start arriving in twos in front of the hotel.

BACK TO: GUNFIGHT

Alabama crawling.

The suitcase full of cocaine is by Dick. Dick grabs it and tosses it in the air. Marvin comes from behind the sofa and fires. The suitcase is hit in mid-air. White powder goes everywhere. The room is enveloped in cocaine.

Dick takes this as his cue and makes a dash out the door.

An IA Officer goes after him.

Lenny makes a break for it.

Wurlitzer goes after him but is pinned down by Marvin.

Alabama reaches the bathroom and finds Clarence.

> ALABAMA

Sweety?

Clarence's face is awash with blood.

> CLARENCE

I . . . I can't see you . . . I've got blood in my eyes . . .

He dies.

Alabama tries to give him mouth-to-mouth resuscitation.

INT. BEVERLY WILSHIRE — HALLWAY — DAY

Dario runs down the hall, right into a cluster of uniformed police.

He fires his shotgun, hitting two, just before the others chop him to ribbons.

INT. BEVERLY WILSHIRE — ANOTHER HALLWAY

The hallway's empty but we hear footsteps approaching fast. Dick comes around the corner, running as if on fire. Then we see the IA Officer turn the same corner.

> IA OFFICER
> (*aiming gun*)

Freeze!

Dick does.

> DICK

I'm unarmed!

> IA OFFICER

Put your hands on your head, you son of a bitch!

He does. Then, from off-screen, a shotgun blast tears into the IA Officer, sending him into the wall.

                           DICK
    Oh shit.

*He starts running again and runs out of frame, then Lenny turns the
corner and runs down the hall.*

*Dick runs into the elevator area, he hits the buttons, he's trapped, it's like
a box.*

Lenny catches up. Dick raises his hands. Lenny aims his sawed-off.

                           DICK
    Look, I don't know who you are, but whatever it was that I did to
    you, I'm so sorry.

Two elevator doors on either side of them open up.

Lenny looks at Dick. He drops his aim and says:

                          LENNY
    Lotsa luck.

*Lenny dives into one elevator car. Dick jumps into the other, just as the
doors close.*

    BACK TO: HOTEL ROOM

*The Mexican stand-off has become two different groups of two pinning
each other down.*

*Wurlitzer has Marvin pinned down behind the sofa and Dimes has Boris
pinned down in the kitchen.*

*In the bathroom, Alabama's pounding on Clarence's bloody chest, trying
to get his heart started. It's not working. She slaps him hard in the face a
couple of times.*

                         ALABAMA
    Wake up, goddamn it!

*Dimes discards his handgun and pulls one of the sawed-off shotguns from
the grip of a dead wise-guy.*

Boris peeks around the wall to fire.

Dimes lets loose with a blast. A scream is heard.

BORIS
(off)

I'm shot! Stop!

DIMES

Throw out your gun, asshole!

The Uzi's tossed out.

Dimes goes to where Wurlitzer is.

DIMES
(to Marvin)

OK, black jacket! It's two against one now! Toss the gun and lie face down on the floor or die like all your friends.

The shotgun's tossed out from behind the sofa.

INT. BEVERLY WILSHIRE — ELEVATOR — DAY

Dick's sitting on the ground, he can't believe any of this. The doors open on the fourth floor. He runs out into the hallway.

HALLWAY

He starts trying the room doors for an open one.

DICK

Oh, God, if you just get me outta this I swear to God I'll never fuck up again. Please, just let me get to *T. J. Hooker* on Monday.

He tries a door, it opens.

STEWARDESS'S ROOM — DAY

Dick steps in. Three gorgeous girls are doing a killer aerobics workout to a video on TV. The music is so loud and they're so into their exercises, they don't hear Dick tiptoe behind them and crawl underneath the bed.

LEE'S ROOM

Boris has caught a lot of buckshot, but he'll live. He's lying on the kitchen floor. Dimes stands over him. He has the sawed-off in his hand.

> DIMES
>
> Don't even give me an excuse, motherfucker.

Dimes pats him down for other weapons, there are none.

Wurlitzer puts the cuffs on Marvin and sits him down on the couch.

Dimes looks in the bathroom and sees the dead Clarence with Alabama crying over him.

Dimes walks over to Wurlitzer.

> DIMES
>
> Everything's under control here.

> WURLITZER
>
> Sorry about Nicholson.

> DIMES
>
> Me too.

> WURLITZER
>
> I'm gonna go see what's goin' on outside.

> DIMES
>
> You do that.

Wurlitzer exits. Dimes grabs the phone.

LOBBY

Shotgun in hand, Lenny moves hurriedly down the lobby.

A Cop yells out.

> COP
>
> You! Stop!

Lenny brings up his sawed-off and lets him have it. Other cops rush forward. Lenny grabs a woman standing by.

> LENNY
>
> Get back or I'll blow this bitch's brains to kingdom come!

Dimes is on the phone talking with the department. Boris is still moaning on the floor. Marvin is sitting on the couch with his hands cuffed behind his back. Alabama is crying over Clarence, then she feels something in his jacket. She reaches in and pulls out his .45 calibre automatic. She wipes her eyes. She holds the gun in her hand and remembers Clarence saying:

CLARENCE
(off)

She's a sixteen-calibre kitten! Equally equipped for killin' an' lovin'! She carried a sawed-off shotgun in her purse, a black belt around her waist, and the white-hot fire of hate in her eyes! Alabama Whitman is Pam Grier! Pray for forgiveness. Rated R . . . for Ruthless Revenge!

Alabama steps out of the bathroom, gun in hand.

Marvin turns his head toward her. She shoots him twice.

Dimes, still on the phone, spins around in time to see her raise her gun. She fires. He's hit in the head and flung to the floor.

She sees Boris on the kitchen floor.

ALABAMA

Bye bye, Boris. Good luck.

BORIS

You too, cutie.

She starts to leave and then spots the briefcase full of money. She takes it and walks out the door.

HALLWAY

The elevator opens and Wurlitzer steps out.

Alabama comes around the corner.

WURLITZER

Hey, you!

Alabama shoots him three times in the belly. She steps into the elevator, the doors close.

LOBBY

Alabama enters the lobby and proceeds to walk out. In the background, cops are all over the place and Lenny is still yelling with the woman hostage.

LENNY

I wanna car here, takin' me to the airport, with a plane full of gas ready to take me to Kilimanjaro and . . . and a million bucks!
(*pause*)
Small bills!

EXT. BEVERLY WILSHIRE – PARKING LOT – DAY

Alabama puts the briefcase in the trunk. She gets into the Mustang and drives away.

INT. MUSTANG – MOVING – DAY

Alabama's driving fast down the freeway. The DJ on the radio is trying to be funny. She's muttering to herself.

ALABAMA

I could have walked away. I told you that. I told you I could have walked away. This is not my fault. I did not do this. You did this one hundred percent to yourself. I'm not gonna give you the satisfaction of feeling bad. I should laugh 'cause you don't deserve any better. I could get another guy like that. I'm hot lookin'. What are you? Dead! Dumb jerk. Asshole. You're a asshole, you're a asshole, you're a asshole. You wanted it all, didn't ya? Didn't ya? Well whatcha got now? You ain't got the money. You ain't got me. You ain't even got your body anymore. You got nothing'. Nada. Zip. Goose egg. Nil. Donut.

The song 'Little Arrows' by Leapy Lee comes on the radio. Alabama breaks down and starts crying. She pulls the car over to the side. The song continues. She wipes her eyes with a napkin that she pulls out of her jacket. She tosses it on the dashboard. She picks up the .45 and sticks it in her mouth.

She pulls back the hammer. She looks up and sees her reflection in the rear-view mirror. She turns it the other way. She look straight ahead. Her finger tightens on the trigger. She sees the napkin on the dashboard. She opens it up and reads it: 'You're so cool.'

She tosses the gun aside, opens up the trunk, and takes out the briefcase. She looks around for, and finally finds, the Sgt Fury comic book Clarence bought her.

And with comic book in one hand, and briefcase in the other, Bama walks away from the Mustang forever.